OUTLAWED!

Jeff Mason thought his troubles were behind him when he rode into Boswell — until he saw his name on a reward poster. With a posse behind him and a bounty hunter ahead, Jeff was beginning to think trouble was his middle name. A greedy sheriff and a couple of deputies looking to cash in on the reward didn't help matters either. Then there was Sanchos. That sneaky, no-good Mex was stirring a wicked brew and no mistake. If he wasn't very careful — and fast — Jeff would finish up between a rock and a hard place.

Books by Clifford H. Fry
in the Linford Western Library:

NORTH TO ABILENE

DM

—
—
.
.
.

CLIFFORD H. FRY

◆

OUTLAWED!

Complete and Unabridged

LINFORD
Leicester

First published in Great Britain in 1996

First Linford Edition
published 2005

The moral right of the author
has been asserted

British Library CIP Data

Fry, Clifford H. (Clifford Henry), *1927 –*
Outlawed!.—Large print ed.—
Linford western library
1. Western stories
2. Large type books
I. Title
823.9′14 [F]

ISBN 1–84395–753–1

Published by
F. A. Thorpe (Publishing)
Anstey, Leicestershire

Set by Words & Graphics Ltd.
Anstey, Leicestershire
Printed and bound in Great Britain by
T. J. International Ltd., Padstow, Cornwall

This book is printed on acid-free paper

1

Jeff Mason rode slowly down the main street of the one-horse town of Boswell.

Over the past two years he'd seen so many small settlements with their clapboard buildings and false frontages. Nothing it seemed was built to last. Just another jumble of buildings, a temporary stopover as the white man pushed ever westward, eating into the Indian territories.

Jeff eased his palomino through the mud of the main street and halted in front of a saloon where, in spite of the recent heavy rains, the batwing doors were continuously flapping backwards and forwards as men entered or left the establishment.

Slipping tiredly from the saddle he looped the reins over the hitching rail, automatically flipping the reins into a second loop which made them easy to release in a hurry, but which would keep the bronc from straying for as long as was necessary.

Jeff stroked the palomino's drooping head. 'Won't be long feller,' he muttered. 'Just a quick look around, an' we'll mosey up to the livery, find you a nice warm stall and get you bedded down.'

The horse blew gently through its nose and shook its head.

Jeff glanced at the line of horses already tied along the rail. 'I know they ain't in your class feller,' he grunted, 'but there ain't no call to get uppity about it so just stick around OK?'

He patted the horse again and stepped up on to the boardwalk heading for the batwings.

The doors flew open and a burly, bewhiskered fellow dressed in workaday overalls and wearing a black bowler hat charged through almost knocking Jeff over.

'Easy there fella,' grunted Jeff, grinning goodnaturedly as he caught the man and held him up until he'd regained his balance. 'That stuff you've bin drinking is making your legs go off on their ownsome.'

The man, obviously a miner from his dress, pushed Jeff away and stared owlishly at the cowboy in front of him.

'You sayin' I can't hold my liquor, mister?' he growled belligerently. ''Cos if you are, you're lookin fer trouble.'

Jeff's face smoothed out; the smile vanished. 'You've just found more than you can handle, mister,' he replied evenly. 'So why don't you just leave it there fer now and come back when you're sober? If you've a mind to.'

The man stared at Jeff for a few moments. His first inclination had been to plant a meaty fist in the young man's face but some sixth sense warned him that it might not be such a good idea.

The badly healed scar over the man's right eye gave an otherwise youthful face a rather sinister twist. The ice-blue eyes had about as much life in them as a piece of flint on a rainy day.

The miner's eyes travelled swiftly downwards over a worn leather jacket and paused on a matched pair of Frontier Colts strapped around a lean, muscular waist.

The miner was sobering fast, but he could not resist waving an admonitory finger under the cowboy's nose. 'You just be more careful in future, sonny,' he growled, 'otherwise . . . '

'If you don't take that finger out of my face right now, *hombre*, I will personally snap it off an' feed it to the vultures,' interrupted Jeff evenly. 'Now move out of my way, fella.'

The man stepped silently to one side. There was a coldness in the pit of his stomach and suddenly he was stone cold sober.

He stumbled off the boardwalk and, as he shambled away, Jeff heard him mutter, 'It took the whole of the mornin' to tie that one on an' he sobered me up in two minutes. What a God-awful waste.'

Jeff watched the miner plod through

the mud as he removed his stetson and used it to dust off his jeans. Replacing his headgear he pushed his way into the crowded saloon and ordered a glass of root beer.

The barkeep, a small wiry-looking man, was one of three, all serving as fast as their hands could fill glasses. His head was completely bald but he had a wealth of side whiskers and a bushy beard. His bright, shoe-button eyes flicked over Jeff as he placed the brimming glass on the bar and collected the ten cents.

'Stopped raining has it?' he asked conversationally.

'Reckon so,' replied Jeff.

'Say, don't I know you from some-where?' asked the barkeep, raising a quizzical eyebrow.

'Depends on where you've been.'

'Oh, I've bin all over,' replied the barman brightly.

'That's a long way.'

'What is?'

'All over,' replied Jeff laconically, as

he strolled away from the bar towards a large notice-board bearing Wanted posters.

'I remember you from som'eres; it'll come to me,' called the barkeep, unabashed.

Jeff scanned the notices absently at first. Then he stiffened, and began to read one of the notices again.

WANTED DEAD OR ALIVE

For robbery and murder at Casa Verde.

Beneath the caption was a description of himself. Jeff could hardly believe his eyes. No wonder the barman thought he'd recognized him, Jeff mused. The man had probably read the description a hundred times.

Jeff glanced quickly towards the bar but there was no sign of the barkeep.

He'd remembered! He'd probably also remembered the $1,000 reward too.

Jeff placed his glass on the nearest

table and headed quickly for the batwings.

With that kind of money on his hide no one would wait to ask questions, and the fact that he'd had nothing to do with the robbery would be difficult to explain after he'd been shot by well-meaning townsfolk.

Jeff paused outside and scanned the roadway. He could see a small group of men striding purposefully towards the saloon, and among them he recognized the barkeep.

Jeff quickly slipped the reins from the tie-rail and led the horse into an alley at the side of the saloon. Taking it around the back of the premises he mounted and rode quietly away.

'Sorry about the grub, old hoss,' he muttered. 'But we'd best put some space twixt them and us *muy pronto*.'

2

That had been three days ago.

Now he rode slumped in the saddle. The sodden J.B. pulled well down against the driving rain which streamed over a slicker that had long since given up trying to protect its wearer from the slashing torrent and the icy cold of the wind.

Bone cold and weary, the horse and rider sloshed through the mud and rain.

He could not understand how or why there was a dodger out on him. It was true that there had been a raid on the bank in Casa Verde. It was also true that he had hunted the gang who had committed the robbery and murder. In fact, the last person to die had been the Mexican, Sanchos Alvarez two years ago, back in the Dakotas.

It was also true that he had never found the body or the money the

Mexican had stolen but he had assumed that the whole matter had been straightened out long ago.

Could it possibly be that Sanchos had once again cheated death when he'd fallen into that chasm?

Something was very wrong and Jeff knew he had to get to Casa Verde before some over-enthusiastic bounty hunter turned him into buzzard meat.

The palomino hardly needed guiding. Somewhere ahead there were trees. It could smell the scent of them on the cutting wind. It told of shelter and, as long as the man on its back did not signal otherwise, it was content to head for the haven.

Jeff Mason had thickened and hardened over the last two years; his body and mind had been forged and tempered in the furnace of life's violence. Violence and a singleness of purpose had built him into a man to be feared.

Sanchos Alvarez. That tricky, sneaky killer must still be alive. Still managing to stay one step ahead of the man he himself had dubbed El Lobo Diablo.

With a price on his head and a posse behind him Jeff dare not seek the warmth of a town.

He squinted ahead at the trees marking the beginnings of a forest. It might be a good place to go to ground, he thought remotely. The posse was not too far behind but perhaps three miserable days of following him, together with another day hunting through the trees dripping with rain might make his pursuers give up.

This could be just the sanctuary he needed.

Jeff guided his willing horse into the protection of the trees, watching his back trail to see how quickly the hoof marks were absorbed by the mud and leaves: He was satisfied that within a few minutes his passing would be obliterated, always providing that his bronc did not decide to leave a 'calling card'. He smiled at the thought. There was no accounting for where a bronc would dump that which it no longer needed.

A figure made dim by the misting rain through the trees watched Mason's progress across the valley floor.

'C'mon friend,' he muttered in savage satisfaction. 'Another hundred yards or so an' I've earned myself a thousand bucks. I can also get outa this damned rain.'

The worn dodger the man carried in his hip pocket was about to pay off he thought as he slid the Winchester from beneath his slicker and snugged the walnut stock to his shoulder.

The sights settled on the slouched figure and the man gently took up the slack on the trigger.

The palomino stumbled on a hidden root in the muck underfoot throwing Jeff violently forward and he grabbed at the saddle horn to avoid being thrown over his mount's head. At the same instant, the killer's reflexes, honed down to a hair trigger, squeezed off his shot.

Jeff felt the pull of the bullet as it clipped through the slicker at his shoulder.

His mind instantly registered. Bushwhack!

Almost without thought he continued his forward movement, allowing himself to tumble into the mud in an ungainly heap. Deliberately he continued his roll until he finished up behind a large boulder.

The palomino looked back at the fallen man and snorted.

'Ah g'wan,' grunted Jeff in disgust, 'I did it on purpose you mangy dog's dinner.' He flipped a dollop of mud at the horse to drive it out of the line of fire.

The man stared into the misty gloom. 'I'm sure I hit the cow-son,' he muttered. 'But did I finish him? He seemed to roll an awful long way fer a dead un'.'

He waited with the patience of an Indian. He'd been a bounty hunter plenty long enough to know better than to go blundering towards a victim who could not be seen. He scanned the area, carefully tracing a passage that would allow him to get behind his quarry.

Fifteen minutes passed on leaden feet and still there was no movement from his victim so the killer decided to follow the path he had mapped out in order to get a good look behind the boulder.

Jeff too was waiting. The slicker had protected his Colts from the mud and he had slowly eased one from its holster. The total lack of movement or sound from the bushwhacker told Jeff that this was no amateur.

It was a Mexican stand-off and neither one could stay in the same place much longer.

The rain had eased off and, as Jeff peered between the dripping foliage, he thought he could discern a darker shadow slipping through the trees towards the trail.

He resisted the temptation to take a shot at the elusive shadow, a tight grin pulling at his mouth. 'I can guess what you're trying to do, mister, so let's see how good you are,' he muttered, as he slid quietly away towards a pile of rocks some twenty feet behind his present position.

It seemed like a mile as he slid through the glutinous mud and, from the smell, mud was only part of it, he thought sourly as he tucked himself tight into the cover.

From this new position Jeff could clearly see the place where he had so recently tumbled from his mount, now it was just a matter of waiting.

He didn't have to wait long before his assailant began methodically to sieve the area where Jeff had been hiding.

Jeff heard his attacker making a rapid reload, and guessed that the man was checking the brush for some sign of movement. He could almost feel the man's indecision, not knowing whether his victim was dead or just wounded. The hunter's sixth sense would be working, trying to assess all the possibilities.

Jeff's lips stretched into a tight humourless grin at the thought. He knew that he would win in any waiting game.

He first saw the top of the man's stetson as it eased above the bushes and he lined his Colt about eighteen inches below it.

Ice-cold, slate-grey eyes watched his attacker's progress with an entire lack of emotion. The hunter was now the hunted and there was no mercy showing in the cold, scarred face.

The muzzle of the Winchester slowly broke through the bushes, followed by a hand and an arm.

With a cold grin of pure malice, Jeff zoned in on the exposed shoulder. 'Right where you almost had me, mister,' he murmured as he squeezed off the shot slamming the man back into the bushes with a scream of agony.

'Real painful, huh?' he continued, as he deliberately planted a second bullet into an exposed leg.

The leg jerked on impact but was not

withdrawn, proving for sure that his unknown enemy was not trying to pull a rusty on him.

Jeff crossed quickly to his unknown assailant. Picking up the Winchester he threw it into the bushes, but he did not bother to remove the Navy Colt that was still snugged tight in the cutaway holster.

Jeff slid tiredly on to a nearby rock to wait for the man to regain consciousness, his pistol hanging loose in one hand, while the other slipped up to the red bandanna bound tightly around his neck, then the hand dropped back under the wet slicker.

The posse must be gaining by leaps and bounds, he thought remotely; he'd have to find some place to lie low, and right soon. Neither he nor his mount was in any fit state to outride them.

The man began to groan as he regained consciousness. He tried rolling over to get up until his eyes focused on the barrel of the ready cocked Colt. It look as big as a cannon from that close.

16

He stopped the cursing and rolling right there.

Jeff knew what the killer would have done if the position had been reversed, and guessed that the man was wondering why he was still alive to think about it.

Sweat and pain showed on the wounded man's face and Jeff could tell from the changing expressions that he was struggling to remain conscious.

'What's your handle this week, fella?' growled Jeff, breaking in on the man's thoughts.

'How come you're askin'?' the man retorted defiantly.

'Got this thing about names, mister,' replied Jeff evenly. 'Like to know what to put in my tally book.'

The throbbing pain was getting to the would-be killer but he was making great efforts to shake it off. 'That damned Mex sold me short,' he grumbled.

'Mex!' snapped Jeff. 'What Mex? What was his name?'

'Said it would be as easy as taking a leak in the crik . . . '

'No creek around here, so that would take some doing,' cut in Jeff laconically. 'Make a deal with you, mister, you tell me the Mexican's name and where you last saw him and I won't bust a cap on you. Seems to me you've got plenty of ventilation in your hide without me giving you another hole up here.' Jeff tapped his pistol against the man's head.

'Done!' he growled eagerly. 'Last I seen him was about twenty miles north of here, place called Stantonville, said he'd hang out there till I collected my pay. Name of Sanchos. Offered me five hundred bucks over and above the reward on the dodger if I took your hair in as proof.'

Jeff crouched beside the wounded man holstering his gun as he did so, allowing his slicker to drop down covering his hands and guns.

The wounded man's eyes turned speculative at Jeff's relaxed manner. 'Is that it, mister?' he asked.

'Not quite; like I said, I have this thing about names an' I still don't know yours. So what's your handle?'

The man's hand had been inching slowly towards his six gun. 'An' that's it, is it?' he asked, a smile beginning to pull at the corner of his mouth.

'That's it!' agreed Jeff casually, apparently ignoring the man on the ground.

The grin widened. 'The name's Riley, Steve Riley.' He almost chuckled as his gun came up for the kill.

Suddenly the smile seemed to freeze; it became fixed as he keeled over.

'Die happy, Mister Riley,' murmured Jeff as he withdrew the wafer-thin blade he kept in a pouch at the back of his neck. He wiped it clean on the man's trouser leg and slipped it back into the sheath behind the bandanna.

'I don't need to put your name in the tally book, Mister Riley, you were just a no-good bounty hunter, but I kept my word, I didn't bust a cap on you. It didn't make any difference in the end though, did it?'

Jeff pushed himself tiredly to his feet, walked over to his palomino and climbed into the saddle.

His suspicions had proved to be true, *Sanchos Alvarez* was still out there somewhere, and only by finding him could he clear the outlaw brand from his name.

He kneed his mount around and started down the trail deeper into the forest.

'Got to find a hidey-hole *pronto* or that darned posse will be breathing down my neck an' you ain't in the mood for a fast run,' he muttered.

On the heels of this observation Jeff heard the not-too-distant thrum of hooves that told of a large body of men moving in his direction.

'Had to go and open my great big mouth didn't I?' he grumbled, as he spurred off the trail and into the bushes, easing his mount forward, coaxing the best out of the tired horse.

Quickly he decided that he would take heed of the words of an old Indian friend: 'Be like the coyote; when in trouble don't run, hide.'

The trees and bushes were much closer now and Jeff noticed an even thicker clump. It looked almost impenetrable but he managed to get his mount through to the middle of the bushes.

Wrapping a small log around the reins he allowed the log to fall to the ground. Jeff knew the horse would stay ground-hitched and not make a sound while it was tethered in this way.

Quickly slipping his Winchester from the saddle boot he pushed his way back through the thicket and rapidly began to backtrack towards the clearing he had so recently left.

Once again Jeff drifted silently into the thickest of the bushes to the left of the trail just before the bedraggled posse began to drift into the clearing.

'Those shots we heard came from up here somewhere,' yelled the sheriff, as he rode ahead of the posse. 'Come on, come on yuh damn lazy layabouts, spread out an' search the area. I don't want that Mason jasper getting away now we're this close.'

One of the posse, a man in a business suit, and obviously someone of importance, shouted irately, 'What the hell's gotten into you, Keever? You're a local sheriff fer God's sake, we've got no jurisdiction way out here. This posse is illegal.'

'Shut your damned mouth, Peters,' retorted Keever. 'I'm the sheriff and if I want a posse to chase an outlaw then I'll damned well have one.'

'You don't even know if this guy's a killer or not,' another posse member complained. 'You're depending on what the barkeep told yuh, an' he could be wrong you know, he only said . . . '

'I *know* what he said,' snapped Keever. 'Now fer God's sake stop whining and start searching. I'm sick to death of your continual moaning and grousing, an' don't forget, shoot on sight, this hairpin's dangerous; now git to it.'

Jeff noticed that all but four of the men were in business clothes or store-keeper's gear, obviously members of the town council impressed into the posse by the sheriff, who was dressed in typical range-rider's gear.

The other three were similarly dressed, each wearing one or two low-slung Colts according to their preference.

Of the whole posse, only these four received the hidden man's critical attention; it would be from these that the first trouble would come. And Jeff had a sure-fire feeling that unless he took a hand, trouble would not be long in coming.

3

Mark Keever called his three henchmen together, 'Listen,' he muttered, 'this lousy mob of fairies ain't gonna do any shooting, yuh kin bet on that, so first sight of the jasper, cut him down.'

'That's a mite drastic, Mark,' grunted Tex Kelso, and Mike Farrier nodded in silent agreement.

'Don't tell me you're goin' soft on us too,' sneered Bret, Mark Keever's younger brother. 'Pr'aps you-all ain't interested in the reward huh? Waal me I like the idea of picking up five thousand dollars from that no-good greaser. Being sworn members of the town's law, me an' Mark can't claim the reward on the dodger, but the five thousand the greaser deposited in the bank sounds like music to me.'

'Yeah,' Mark chimed in. 'An' if one of you two should claim to have shot the hairpin, you can claim the reward on the dodger as well, that'll make six thousand to share four ways. Sound good to you fellas?'

'Waal let's start lookin',' agreed Tex, with a nod to Mike Farrier. 'Let's go wake up our posse of old ladies and make sure they keep searching.'

The majority of the posse was disconsolately searching at the sides of the trail when there was a signal shot.

'Over here!' shouted one of the men from around the bend in the trail, and with one accord the men hurried up the trail. All that is, except Roland Potter, old Roly-Poly as he was sneeringly known by the hardcases in town. He had not raised any objection at all, nor was he about to follow the general migration towards the pistol shot.

'Oh no!' big, fat Roland Potter told his bronc loudly. 'If that's where they expect to find the killer, then we might as well go the opposite way, and kinda sneak up on him like, from the rear.'

With this blithe statement made,

Roland Potter allowed his bronc to amble directly towards the clump of bushes hiding the man they all sought.

He spurred his reluctant mount into the bushes, and straight into the barrel of Mason's Winchester.

'Oh my good God,' he squeaked. 'We done found him.'

'Shuddup and slide off,' snarled Jeff. 'Or so help me I'll blow your God-damned head off.'

'Now don't git *hasty*,' stammered Roly. 'Dammit, I wasn't even *looking*, an' it had to be me that finds you.'

'Your hard luck, mister, now shut your gabby mouth an' slide off *pronto*.'

Roly half fell off his mount in his eagerness to please and quickly pushed his hands into the air as if trying hard to grab some of the low-hanging cloud.

'Wh-what are you gonna do with me?' he stuttered.

Jeff had been searching for an answer to that one ever since he'd realized that the fat man was going to discover his hiding place. For, as tough as he

26

pretended to be, there was no way he could cause harm to the trembling tub of lard in front of him.

The guy was so scared it was almost funny . . . almost.

'How come you're riding with that bunch, you don't seem like a posse-man to me?'

'Oh I *know*,' sighed Roly. 'Er, do you mind if I put my hands down? I'm not built for this sort of thing, d'you see. I fit into a rocker so much better, with a tall glass of something cool preferably.'

Jeff inclined his head. 'OK, but . . . '

'I do assure you, sir,' Roly interrupted, 'you have nothing whatsoever to fear from me, I would not even *dream* of attempting to disarm you, dear me no.'

Jeff allowed himself a small grin. 'No, I guess not, but you still ain't told me what you're doin' with that posse.'

'Believe me, sir, *I* don't know what I'm doing here either; in fact I don't know what any of us are doing here.

We're miles outside the sheriff's jurisdiction and most of the members have complained of this from time to time. I don't even understand the sheriff's sudden zeal, he rarely gets off his butt most days. Now, suddenly, he has us chasing all over creation, just because some joker said you were a mad-dog killer. Very commendable of him you understand, but all very unusual.'

'Sounds almost as if he was getting paid for it,' muttered Jeff. 'And I don't mean the money the town's paying him either.' Jeff surveyed the plump, frightened man through narrowed eyes. 'You're gonna have to tell your sheriff that you've had enough; in fact you're gonna spit in his eye and tell him you ain't goin' a single step further, an' he can do what he damn-well likes about it.'

'What *me*?' squeaked Roly, aghast. 'I . . . I'm gonna say *that*!'

'That's right, that's just what you're gonna do.'

'Are you *mad*? I am not going to do any such thing. No sir! *No, no, no!*'

'So die then,' gritted Jeff. 'Right now!'

'All right, *All right*! Don't get so hasty with that God-damned gun,' stuttered Potter, rolling his eyes tragically. 'I will definitely defy Sheriff Keever, er . . . *how?*'

'Now listen carefully, this ain't gonna be so hard as it seems.'

'You are joking, of course.'

'He can't do anything to you in front of all those witnesses, can he! He'll probably shout a lot and threaten, but that'll be all one big bluff, he daren't shoot you.'

'D'you think I could possibly have your written guarantee of that?' interrupted Roly, his voice trembling in tune with his body.

'No, but look at it this way, while he can't I can, and what's more I *will. Comprende?*'

'Oh dear me, yes, indeed I do!'

'Please don't doubt me, my fat

friend,' continued Jeff evenly. 'Remember, a man your size makes a pretty easy target.'

'That's always been my trouble,' wailed Roly. 'So, what shall I do?'

'You just take your bronc back through the bushes and sit on that big log over there, right where I can see you, and when he comes looking you tell him you ain't moving another God-damned inch, an' he can go plumb to Hell in a bucket for all you care. Oh, by the way, if you do decide to move you'll wake up in Hell, because my rifle will be aimed at the back of your head. Got it?'

'Oh yes, yes indeed. I sit on that log and — and I tell Sheriff Keever t-to go t-to Hell in a b-b-bucket. Er, couldn't we phrase it in rather softer tones?'

'On your way, fella,' replied Jeff. 'And remember . . .'

'I know, *I know*! One wrong move and . . . oh my God.'

Roly grabbed frantically at the reins and pushed his way back out of the thicket. He could feel a burning sensation at the nape of his neck. He didn't like what he had to do but he liked the cold-eyed man behind him even less.

'He *meant* it too,' he told his bronc earnestly. 'That's the trouble with being fat, it makes it so hard to *miss*!'

He squatted on the fallen tree like a man under the death sentence clutching desperately at the reins of his mount, hoping that Sheriff Keever would fall and break his stupid neck or something, anything that would save him from saying what that man back there had told him to say.

Roly's tragic thoughts were interrupted by another pistol shot.

Maybe somebody has shot the sheriff he thought hopefully. His face brightened at the thought only to make it even more melancholy when he thought that Sheriff Keever was probably doing the shooting.

'Oh my God, the things I get into. I wouldn't *mind*, but I don't even *try* to

31

get into these scrapes,' he muttered
dejectedly.

The shot had been fired by a posse
member who had stumbled upon
Riley's body and it soon brought the
rest of the men to the spot.

Scowling, the sheriff pushed his way
through the group of men to stare
down at the body.

'Looks kinda like we found the jasper
at last,' growled one of the men. 'Now,
perhaps we can get back to our
businesses and stop traipsing all over
the God-damned landscape.'

Keever's scowl stayed right where it
was however. He knew that this was not
the man they were searching for.

He signalled for his brother and his
other two cronies to follow him away
from the rest of the men.

'Think we can git away with it?' he
muttered.

'Get away with what?' asked Tex.

'Waal, if the rest of 'em think it's that
Mason feller and we agree, we could
bury him right here in front of

witnesses and collect our dough from that greaser.'

'You reckon we could pull a rusty like that an' git away with it?' asked his brother, his voice rising in derision.

'Keep your darned voice down,' snarled the sheriff. 'I don't want the whole damned posse to hear you squawking.'

'It's no go,' grunted Tex. 'You just ain't thought about it enough, Mark. This Mason joker will be turning up again sooner or later, then what's gonna happen?'

'Yeah, an' I don't wanna be around when the muck starts flying,' enjoined Bret Keever.

'Know what I think?' asked Mike Farrier, of no one in particular.

'Do tell,' growled the sheriff. 'Everybody else is having their two-cents' worth so let's hear you rabbit for a spell.'

'Well, I could be wrong of course . . . '

'I just bet you could,' interrupted Keever, sarcastically.

Farrier stared at the sheriff and Keever was first to break the stare.

'As I was sayin',' continued Farrier. 'I reckon the dead guy was another of the greaser's safety plans, until he met up with this Mason hairpin an' his knife. Then another little plan bit the dust.'

'Yeah, that's it!' ejaculated Tex. 'That's just about a sneakin' greaser's mark.'

'Hmm,' muttered the sheriff thoughtfully, 'that makes sense, but that means we must be mighty close to the damned lobo wolf. Let's git the posse back on the trail and make a search of this whole area. We could have the jasper in a couple of hours.'

'That's what I like about this chase,' sneered his brother. 'Plenty of very definite maybes and a few very certain probablys, but so far we ain't seen hide nor hair of the bastard, an' I got an awful feeling that if and when we *do* catch sight of him we ain't gonna like it one little bit.'

Still arguing among themselves they

made their way back to the main bunch of men who were still collected around the body.

'OK everybody, let's get back on the trail,' shouted Keever. 'We're gonna search this whole damned area.'

'Ain't we gonna bury this feller then?'

'Look at it this way,' replied Keever, his voice dripping sarcasm. 'Did he *say* just where he wanted to be buried? No! So who am I to bury him in the wrong place! Now, git back to the search and shut up.'

Muttering and grumbling the posse slipped and stumbled back towards their mounts.

They drew to a halt when they saw Roland Potter sitting on the fallen tree just as he had been instructed.

The men nudged each other and some even managed a tired grin or two.

'What's old Potter thinking of?' muttered one. 'Keever will have his fat hide for breakfast if he sees him.'

'I'd eat anything myself,' muttered the other as Keever approached.

The sheriff was beginning to think that half the world was against him, and that the other half wasn't all that chummy either. Seeing Roly lazing around on the tree like a big fat bullfrog as if he had all the time in the world was more than just waving a red rag at a bull. It was like waving the bull at the rag.

'What the cotton-pickin' hell do you think you're doing!' he yelled. 'S'you think this is a God-damned picnic, you fat slob?'

Potter's mind cringed from what he now had to do. He didn't even try to move; he couldn't have anyway. His inner manhood, long dormant, struggled with his fear and his desperate plight gave him a new-found courage. Most people had one choice in two, he didn't have any.

Potter took a huge gulp of air. 'No, Sheriff,' he replied with some spirit. 'I do not think this is a picnic. In fact, I, along with many others here, know damned well it's anything *but* a picnic.

It's more like a wild goose chase, which you, for some obscure reason seem determined to go on with, regardless of anyone or anything. I hereby inform you that I, for one, intend to go no further.'

A stunned silence greeted the end of the rather long speech and Roland Potter felt the sweat popping on his face and dribbling down his many chins. Who said it was cold? he thought miserably, yet he still had time to wonder at his outward calm.

A mutter of surprised agreement came from most of the posse.

'You tell him, Roly,' muttered one of the men from the rear of the crowd.

'Yeah, we're all fed up to the back teeth,' growled another.

Keever, still getting over the shock, managed to find his voice at last. 'Why damn your mangy hide,' he almost screamed. 'Git up offen that damned log and move yourself. We go or stay when I say so an' not before. Now move it or I'll put a slug in your fat ass.'

Keever drew his gun giving added weight to his threat.

Roland Potter was surprised at himself, mostly because he was no longer afraid. Keever's gun was waving in his general direction but he knew that the sheriff would not commit himself in front of all these witnesses, so the gun waving was just so much bluff.

That's it, thought Roly in great surprise, Keever was just a great big noise. A very real danger with no witnesses about, but here and now he could do no more than bluster.

This was Roly Potter's day and he decided to push Keever to the limit.

'Like I said, Sheriff, I'm staying put, what the others intend to do is up to them.'

Angry murmurs came from the posse members.

'I agree with Potter,' growled one. 'Move over, Roly, an' make room fer me.'

Potter didn't move. For while he was now sure that Keever was bluffing he had no such thoughts about the cold-eyed man hiding somewhere behind him.

He kept his voice level. 'I said I ain't moving until I'm ready, so if you wanna sit, then sit. There's plenty of room on this here log without moving me.'

'OK, OK,' protested the man. 'Don't get so all-fired uppity. I'm on your side, remember?'

One after the other the disgruntled men squatted on or near the log, seemingly needing Potter's protection for their decision, until only Keever, his brother and his two henchmen were left standing.

'If you're in a hurry, Sheriff, let's not detain you,' Potter said with a condescending air. 'Oh and don't bother to return to Boswell, I think I speak for everyone here when I say we need another sheriff to represent our town in future.'

There were murmurs of agreement from the men. They'd had more than enough of Keever's domineering ways.

For a moment the ex-sheriff contemplated blasting Potter into oblivion; it showed in his hand reflexes but his brother quickly grabbed his arm. 'Easy there Mark. Put that damned gun away,' he muttered. 'D'you wanna git us all on dodgers fer murder?'

'Yeah, let's ride,' growled Tex. 'Afore we get more trouble than we kin handle.'

Mark Keever shook his brother's hand from his arm, his anger and impatience showing as he pushed the gun savagely into its holster.

'Yeah, OK we're going.' He pointed a finger at Potter. 'But mark this, I'll be bringing that lobo wolf in dead or alive and, as I am no longer the sheriff of Boswell, I shall expect to get the reward on his hide. You try to stop me in that, Potter, and I'll kill you.'

He turned to his three henchmen. 'C'mon, we'll soon find the jasper; we don't need this bunch of store-keepers.'

The four men backed away from the rest of the men, picked up the trailing reins and swung aboard their mounts. 'Remember what I said, Potter, git in my way agin an' they'll be burying you.'

At the last moment Keever snatched up the trailing reins of the pack horse.

'I'll take this to make up for the pay the town owes me,' he shouted, as the four men whirled their mounts and rode off.

'Phew,' muttered Peters. 'I thought they were going to start a war here for a moment.'

'They've taken the damned food though,' moaned Potter: 'We should have stopped 'em.'

'Saying we should have stopped them and doing it is two different things,' replied Peters. 'You sure stood up to 'em, but I think that trying to dictate terms would have carried it just too far and we really would have had a shooting war on our hands.'

'Maybe,' agreed Potter magnanimously.' Then he raised his voice. 'Right men,' he almost shouted. 'Are we all agreed that we ride straight back to Boswell?'

'Well yeah,' replied one of the men. 'There's no need to shout, Roly, we kin hear you OK.'

'Is it all agreed then? OK let's *go*!' he almost bellowed, hoping to God that the man behind him with the rifle would clearly understand. He stood up and waited for the bullet to enter the back of his head.

It didn't happen so he grinned expansively at his friends and swung laboriously aboard his mount, followed by the rest of the men, who were all congratulating him for his courage in standing up to Keever and his bunch.

Basking in their admiration was entirely new to Roland Potter; they usually treated him with a type of almost respectful contempt, so he was not about to tell anyone that he had been forced into confronting Keever and his bunch of gunmen, he liked basking in glory for a change.

4

Jeff watched the men ride off with mixed feelings. If it had not been for Keever and his cronies Jeff would have surrendered himself to the posse and would have taken a chance on their sense of fairness. But having already dealt with one bounty hunter today, Jeff was not about to put his life in the hands of Keever and his pards.

His mind was still in a turmoil over Sanchos and he knew that he must go back to Casa Verde as soon as possible to clear his name.

Jeff flitted silently from tree to tree until he reached the thicket where he had hidden his mount.

He was about to force his way into the bushes when he noticed a footprint slowly filling with silt and water; another two or three minutes and the mark would have been obliterated.

He heard his mount blow through its nose and stamp its feet, a sure sign that it was restless. It had been disturbed!

Jeff slipped quietly into the bushes while he formulated a plan.

His horse had obviously been discovered by Keever and his bunch and they were waiting somewhere close for him to go into the thicket to collect his mount. But for that one tell-tale footprint he would have fallen into the trap.

Jeff lay his Winchester on the ground and quietly removed his slicker. Rolling it into a tight ball he pushed it into the scrub at the base of the bushes.

He eased his guns in their holsters, then picking up his rifle he began to circle the area, flitting from tree to tree like a shadow.

Daylight was fading fast and Jeff wanted to discover where the men were hiding before darkness fell.

He heard a scuffed foot on leaves as one of the men grew restless, and the hoarse curse of another telling the restless one to keep still.

Jeff moved on. He ghosted up to two trees growing from the same base and paused there. Jeff could smell stale tobacco and he realized that someone was close; although the man was not smoking now, Jeff could smell it on the clothes he wore.

There was a slight movement directly in front of him and Jeff discerned a stetson between the two trees. The man's back was resting in the base of the V and his head was lolling between the two trees as he stared forward towards the restless palomino.

It was too good a chance to miss. Jeff's Colt moved up and down in a swift arc and the man slumped forward without a sound.

Pushing the man over Jeff moved silently into his place. He slipped his sixgun into its holster tilted his stetson over his eyes and allowed his Winchester to lie against his body. The seemingly indolent way he was sitting belied his tense readiness for instant action.

Jeff allowed his eyes to wander from point to point; there was still one other man to be accounted for.

He looked across to where he knew the other two were hiding, which was about a quarter of the way around the tiny clearing. He made an educated guess that the third man would be almost opposite his own position. If he had stepped into the clearing he would have been caught in a lethal crossfire.

Jeff could see his mount as a darker blob in the centre. He contemplated the possibility of sneaking forward and driving it out of danger. Unfortunately his horse was so well trained that he knew it would not move while it was ground-hitched to the tiny log.

Jeff stared hard at the position opposite. Somewhere over there the fourth man waited, so he slipped back into the forest.

Tex Kelso stared at the horse in front of him and fingered the trigger of his carbine restlessly. He was a man of action; not for him this pussyfooting in the trees. When he set out to kill a guy he liked to get it done.

He needed a smoke bad, had done for some time. He slipped behind a tree and fished the makings out of his pocket. It took but a few seconds to twist a quirley into shape. Pushing close to the tree he cupped his hands around the lucifer as he drew it across the barrel of his carbine.

The flare of the match hardly showed so carefully did he cup the match between his two palms, but Jeff caught the momentary flicker of light before it was quickly extinguished.

This time Jeff did not want silence. He wanted a diversion. He flicked the rifle to his shoulder and fired three rapid shots.

Kelso cursed luridly as bark from the tree spattered into his face. He grabbed for his carbine as a bullet smashed the cigarette from his mouth taking some of his lip with it.

Kelso dived for the ground. He could feel the blood running into his mouth muffling his curses. The pain was excruciating. He stared wildly around as two more shots smacked earth into his face.

His night vision had gone, destroyed by the flaring light of the match. He could barely see the flash of the gun shooting at him but he shot back anyway in a wild effort of self-defence.

The shots allowed Jeff to pick his target.

Kelso felt a bullet tug at his boot, the second ripped across his neck. He didn't feel the third: It took away the top of his head.

Almost as the last shot left the rifle Jeff was moving back around the circle. He could hear the other two men charging through the trees like a herd of buffalo. He stood completely still as they thundered past towards where their fourth man had been posted.

After they had blundered by, Jeff flitted silently across the clearing and led his horse to safety.

Keever must have found their man because moments later Jeff heard him call for 'someone to shoot the hairpin's horse'. 'He's som'eres close,' Jeff heard him yell.

Jeff smiled grimly in the darkness. 'They left it a mite late, old hoss,' he muttered. 'One down, three to go.'

As he broke out on to the main trail a horse whinnied. Jeff turned the palomino towards the sound. The pack horse had been tied to a tree while Keever and his partners had been searching for him.

A big grin spread across Jeff's face, changing it instantly from the face of a rather formidable man to boyishness.

'Well, well, hoss, looks like they're even providing the grubstake,' he grinned, as he untied the reins and gigged his mount into a trot towing the pack-horse behind him.

Jeff rode steadily onward through the greater part of the night intending to put as much space as he could between himself and his pursuers before he satisfied the hunger gnawing deep within him.

Dawn was tinging the horizon when Jeff eventually discovered a small cave. It was so obscured by foliage that he almost rode past it.

There was also a small coulée nearby with good grass for the two horses.

Jeff close hobbled the pack horse just in case it should stray, but he stripped the saddle and bridle from the palomino so that it could roam freely, knowing it would come when called.

He dumped the gear, together with the packs of food, in the cave then set about preparing a meal over a small smokeless fire concealed within some rocks he had collected and stacked in the back of the cave under a narrow shaft reaching up into the rocks.

The meal over he lay back relaxing in the luxury of the fire's warmth, a pleasant change from the long, cold ride. Many times through the ride he had longed for the protection of his

50

slicker which was still tucked under the brush where he had left it.

The warmth made him feel comfortable, drowsy and safe; his eyes became heavy and he was soon fast asleep.

5

Mark Keever was in a foul mood and his brother Bret was not exactly feeling bright either. The swelling on the back of his head was throbbing like hell, and the looks of quiet contempt from Mike Farrier didn't help a bit.

'If I could only get within touching distance of the cow-son, I'd make him sorry,' growled Bret aggrievedly.

'You damn well did,' sneered his brother. 'An' you got one hell of a lump to prove it. So what did you do? Nothin'! That's what.'

'The guy was like a cat,' Bret excused himself. 'Didn't hear a whisper, then pow! an' the lights went out.'

'An' you told me your kid brother was good,' sneered Mike Farrier. 'He ain't safe to be let out on his own.'

'You were as bad,' snarled Mark. 'I

told you to shoot his damned hoss, but did you?'

'I keep telling you,' replied Farrier. 'The bronc was already gone. The damned lobo wolf had already slipped in and out of the clearing an' none of us saw him do it.'

Still arguing they collected their mounts and swung aboard. 'Go an' git the pack-horse, Bret,' snarled Mark. 'We'll get some grub and start again in the mornin'.'

Bret peeled off and rode back to where they had left the pack-horse only to return a few moments later cursing and swearing.

'Now what's up! Git the pack-horse, I said. Can't you even do that?' snarled Mark.

'Ain't no pack-hoss,' growled Bret. 'The hairpin's traipsed off with our grub, so now what are we gonna do?'

'Wait till daylight then follow his trail,' muttered Mark determinedly. 'Nobody, but nobody pulls this kind of stunt on Mark Keever an' gets away with it. I'm gonna pin that hairpin's carcass to a tree an' the quicker the better. What say you, Mike?'

Farrier nodded. 'You taking the kid along?'

'Who are you calling a kid? Don't make me do something I might regret,' snarled Bret.

'If you don't take your hand from that gun, fella, you'll be regretting it *muy pronto*,' replied Mike evenly.

'Will you two broncos stop ridin' each other,' Mark shouted. 'Save the bullets fer that Mason jasper. Now, come on, let's try to get some rest. We want to be on the trail at first light.'

'I'm hungry, an' I can't sleep when I'm hungry,' growled Bret.

'So stay awake,' replied his brother in disgust.

'Pity he didn't do that when he was supposed to be watching earlier,' sneered Farrier.

'This guy was going to be so easy!' growled Bret Keever as he followed the other two down the trail. 'Just tell me again how easy it was gonna be, Mark, so I can die laughing.'

'Somebody is gonna die,' snarled his brother viciously, 'but it won't be from laughing. Lead poisoning more like.'

'Do tell,' griped Bret. 'God knows we've had enough chances to punch his ticket but he's still out there causing us grief.'

'Yeah? Well this time he's shot his bolt. Now shut your grumbling an' grow up fer Christ sake; I'm sick to death of your moaning.'

6

It was high noon when Jeff was aroused by some foreign sound picked up by his innate sixth sense.

He lay there for a moment without moving, allowing his eyes to take a quick inventory of his surroundings. He could sense nothing wrong within the cave but knew something had disturbed him.

Jeff came erect in one silent, fluid motion, his body giving no sign of stiffness from sleeping several hours on the rocky floor.

He eased his Colts in their holsters before picking up his rifle and checking the loads.

The noise came again, horses' hooves on rock!

Jeff slipped to the hidden opening. He could hear the sounds of horses but they were neither approaching nor leaving the area, which had to mean the horses were tethered close by.

Before he had time to slip away, the bushes were being pushed apart and bullets began to ping and whine around him, making him retreat rapidly into the back of the cave with bullets still humming like angry hornets as they ricocheted from the rocky walls.

Jeff had already checked the cave for other exits before deciding to make use of it. There was only one: the narrow chimney under which he had made his fire.

Bullets were still being poured into the cave, the men outside satisfied to stay out there in safety knowing that sooner or later one of the wildly flying missiles would bring him down.

Laying his rifle on top of the rest of his gear, he ducked into the narrow opening and began to climb.

As he did so he silently prayed to his Indian protector to make sure the narrow opening would allow him to climb all the way to the top. Jeff could think of nothing worse than becoming stuck halfway up the narrow funnel of rock.

He dimly realized that the shooting had stopped as he pulled himself slowly upward, his shoulders almost jamming in the opening. If they should decide to enter the cave now he would be caught, as helpless as a fly in a web.

A voice he recognized as the sheriff's floated up to him. 'Hey, you in there, We're here to arrest you an' take you back to Boswell. You'll git a fair trial if you come quietly; if not we'll blast you out. You listenin', *hombre?*'

Jeff made sure his feet were well placed, then he leaned back, resting his shoulders against the wall. Hanging on with one hand he carefully drew one of his Colts. He was prepared to sell himself dearly if they chanced to look into the funnel.

'Reckon he's dead already,' another voice said. 'Let's rush him; there's three of us fer God's sake.'

Then a third voice complaining that

58

'the jasper might be waiting for them to do just that', prompted an idea that might give him enough time to get out of the chimney.

'Why don't you come and get me?' he shouted, then fired three shots down the chimney, slipped his gun into its holster, and began climbing with renewed vigour as the men below began to pour more shots into the empty cave.

Jeff pulled himself out of the chimney and into the harsh sunlight with a sigh of relief, and not a moment too soon either he thought, as a bullet came ricocheting up through the shaft followed by a voice, bewailing the fact he had managed to elude them yet again.

He lay there a moment intending to catch his breath when he heard Keever's voice cursing their luck.

Jeff grinned at their cursing. The grin died, however, when he heard the sheriff snarl, 'Right, we'll show the bastard. His hoss must be about here somewhere, find it and cut its damned throat. We'll put him afoot, then let's see him get away.'

The voices faded as the men left the cave and Jeff leapt to his feet.

He had to find a way down into the valley and fast before Keever and his gang carried out their threat.

He'd had the palomino as a colt years ago, a gift from his Indian friend, Eagle Eye. Horse and boy had grown up together.

Jeff replaced the spent bullets in his Colt as he ran, leaping from rock to rock like a mountain lion as he rapidly descended into the valley. His only thought was for the safety of the palomino.

He heard a flurry of hooves ahead of him and the curses of men being thwarted as they tried to trap the horse.

Jeff heard the shrill whinny he recognized so well. The breath was rasping in his throat with the effort of his run.

He heard the almost simultaneous crash of three rifles and a whinny that was cut off suddenly.

Jeff stopped his headlong run and stood sagging in the middle of the trail. So close to his mount yet so far away when the horse he loved needed him most.

The sob throbbing in Jeff's throat was not from the breakneck run. He released a high, keening Indian death note of sorrow and regret.

Jeff knew instinctively that his friend of many years was dead. His one tenuous hold with the past was gone forever, now he had nothing to cling to, nothing that was . . . except vengeance.

★　★　★

In those few moments Keever and his men could have killed Jeff with ease, but they were far too busy gloating over the fact that they had put their quarry at a great disadvantage. He was afoot and many miles from the nearest town. It would be just a matter of time now before they ran him to earth.

They laughed and slapped each other on the back.

'We could do with some meat fer supper,' laughed the sheriff. 'Nice piece of haunch should cook well, eh?'

'Yeah,' grinned Mike Farrier. He turned to Bret Keever. 'What's up with you, kid? You look about as happy as an undertaker in a ghost town.'

'Yeah, well, you can laugh but I ain't eating any of that nag, I got the God-damndest feeling the *hombre*'s watchin' us; he just ain't natural somehow.'

Uneasily, they all gazed around at the concealing trees and bushes, each fingering the triggers of their rifles.

'Ah,' growled his brother, still uneasy. 'You're just letting him git to you, kid, he ain't nowhere around.'

'Yeah?' responded Bret. 'Well, what in hell was that God-awful yell we heard just now? Seemed all around us somehow. I'm tellin' yuh, Brother, he's out there, an' we ain't huntin' him. He's gonna be huntin' us.'

'Aw come on,' grunted Farrier hesitantly. 'Don't be putting a hex on us now, Bret, we're three to one. We can ride out any time we like an' leave him stranded; he'd die out here in three days.'

'But you can feel it too huh?' queried Bret.

'Yeah, kinda. Weird ain't it?'

'Well, *I* don't feel nothin',' snarled Mark Keever savagely. 'An' I don't mind eating a nice piece of hossflesh fer supper.'

He drew his Bowie knife and held it aloft. 'I'm gonna cut me a slice,' he said, his voice dripping sarcasm. 'Are you two old ladies gonna join me?'

The shot spun the knife out of his grasp and sent them all diving for protection behind the dead horse as they levered shells into their rifles and poured a concentrated fire into the scrub where a slight whiff of smoke revealed the attacker's hiding place.

'Not around, huh?' gritted Bret. 'Then who the hell was *that*?'

No one answered as they reloaded and continued to sieve the bushes as fast as they could depress triggers.

In the pause that followed a second reload, Mark Keever called for a ceasefire.

'We're using fifty shots to his one shooting at shadows,' he snarled. 'We'll soon be out of shells at this rate.'

They lay there for a short while in silence.

'I reckon the sneaking sonofabitch is long gone,' Keever continued. 'He fires one shot an' we empty our magazines at a shadow.'

He raised his head slightly until his eyes were just above the line of the horse's flank.

On the heels of the shot his stetson flicked savagely to one side bringing sharp curses from the sheriff as he yanked his head back into cover and the trio scrabbled along the flank of the horse for protection from this new position of fire.

'Gone huh,' grunted his brother in

obvious disgust. 'The bastard's got us pinned down a treat. Ain't no way we kin get from here to the trees without him pokin' us full of holes.'

'He's only using a Colt,' grunted Farrier. 'We've got the beating of him with our carbines.'

'Yeah, right!' replied Bret Keever sarcastically. 'But we can't damn-well see him can we, while he can sit in the bushes an' play target practice with us just whenever he likes!'

A third shot came from a different direction and Bret let out a yell as the bullet snapped off the heel of his boot making him snatch his exposed feet into the doubtful protection of the dead horse as once again they scrabbled into a new position.

'Spread some lead around,' snarled Mark Keever. 'We're here till sunset so let's not make things too easy fer the sidewinder. Let's make him realize what he's up against.'

'Oh believe me, he *knows*!' growled his brother. 'An' I know which side *I'd* like to be on right about now too.'

'No point in just wasting cartridges,' muttered Farrier. 'Best keep watching the scrub; anything moves, shoot.'

By tacit agreement they each took a section and scanned backwards and forwards until their eyes ached and jumpy nerves made them fire at every movement.

7

After the third shot Jeff left the area and made his way back to the cave.

He had stifled his grief at the loss of the palomino and was already planning his revenge.

Jeff quickly gathered up his rifle, saddle gear and the food packs. He knew from the conversation he had overheard that the three men would not leave the protection of the dead horse until after dark so he utilized the time to find himself another niche where he quickly provided himself with a meal.

Then, making sure that the fire was completely out, he carried the gear to a rocky outcrop several hundred yards from where he had eaten.

Removing his lariat and pushing the packs, saddle and Winchester deep into some scrub he rolled rocks in front of it then scattered dead leaves over and among them.

He surveyed the area critically for a few moments before deciding that he had left no sign of a recent disturbance. Collecting the lariat and checking his Colts he moved off into the darkening night.

It was time to plan his revenge for the senseless slaughter of his palomino.

Jeff ghosted up to the edge of the small clearing. The dead horse showed as a darker blob, but there were no buzzards around, a sure sign that the men had not yet left the spot.

He lay flat on his stomach so that he could highlight any movement against the lighter backdrop of the night sky.

One by one the three cautiously eased to their feet. Keeping crouched over to make as small a target as possible they ran for the cover of the trees.

Smiling grimly in the darkness, Jeff also stood up and moved silently towards his quarry, keeping close behind them as they hurried towards the cave. He waited until they had entered the cave before quickly scaling the rocks so that he was above the opening. The cursing of the disgruntled men when they found that the stores had gone, more than covered any slight noise he made.

Jeff finally stopped some twelve feet above the cave entrance. Standing with his back to the rock, he watched as the three came out below him, still arguing.

'OK, OK,' snarled the sheriff. 'So we made a mistake back there. Who was willing to stick his stupid head up to find out if the cow-son was still around?'

No one replied. 'Yeah,' continued Keever. 'An' that's how I felt about it too.'

'I figger we'd best stop arguing with each other and git organized,' remarked Farrier without heat. 'Might be a good idea to check on the horses. We've killed his nag so what's to stop him takin' ours while we've bin playin' hide and go seek behind that dead nag of his?'

'Yeah,' grunted Bret Keever, real worry in his voice. 'I told yuh! He's huntin' us, not t'other way round. That sneaking swine could leave *us* afoot.'

'Makes sense,' replied his brother. 'Bret, you stay here just in case the sneaky varmint decides to come back fer some reason. We'll go an git the broncs, then we'll really start hunting that damned lobo wolf.'

'Bet he's plumb shakin' in his boots,' replied Bret sarcastically to no one in particular, as the other two left. 'Us tough *hombres* all huntin' him at once, sure must be frightening.'

That was when the lariat whispered down over his head and snatched tight under his chin leaving him choking and gurgling as Jeff hauled him off his feet and cinched the rope around the bole of a tree.

Jeff climbed down from the rocks and stared at the choking man as he scrabbled at the noose. 'Collar kinda tight is it?' he asked quietly. 'I figger it's enough to git a feller all choked up,' he finished, as the man's feet kicked twice more before dangling uselessly limp.

Jeff turned away without a further glance. 'Two down, two to go,' he muttered quietly as he climbed back up the slope to where he had cinched the lariat.

Balancing himself carefully on a ledge he hauled the dead body some ten feet off the ground. Against the side of the rocky face the body was almost invisible.

Jeff made a loop in the lariat and fitted it over a rock to keep the body in position then he sat back and waited for the return of the sheriff and Mike Farrier.

Twenty minutes passed before Jeff heard the clop of horses' hooves heralding the return of the two men.

Farrier pushed his way through the screening hedge and stared around. He sensed trouble and his sixgun seemed to jump into his hand as he backed cautiously through the bushes again.

Jeff heard him call for his partner and in a few moments the two men returned. Both were two-gun men and the weak moon glinted dully on the weapons in their hands.

'Bret, where are yuh?' called his brother in a hoarse whisper.

Jeff watched immobile, the wafer-thin knife in his hand as the two dark shadows cautiously approached the cave's mouth.

'Likely he's heard somethin' an' gone searching,' muttered Keever.

'Wandered off more like,' replied Farrier with a sneer in his voice.

'He'd better not have,' answered Keever. 'I'll kick his stupid ass when I find him.' He raised his voice to a kind of whispering shout. 'Bret, yuh blamed fool, show yourself; quit actin' the goat, damn you.'

They were standing directly in front of the cave mouth as Jeff cut the lariat and the body plummeted down in front of them.

Four shots rang out as the startled

pair reacted instinctively to what they thought was an attack.

The two waited a moment in the aftermath of the shots until their night sight returned, then Keever moved forward cautiously and nudged the recumbent form with his foot before dropping to his knees to explore the body. He began to curse when he realized just who they had shot.

'You no good, stupid sonofabitch,' he muttered. 'What did you do a stupid thing like that for?'

Farrier had also dropped to his knees beside the body. 'We didn't kill him,' he muttered. 'We just filled him full of lead; he was dead already, Mark. Look at the rope around his neck, that sneakin' lobo wolf done fer him a'fore we got back here. Maybe we should have left the bronc alone an' rode on our way like Bret wanted to, huh?'

'Yeah? Well, I'm still here an' I don't intend tuh let him git away with killin' my brother. He may have been a smart ass, but he *was* my brother fer Christ sake. That hairpin is gonna find out that I'm one *hombre* that makes pretty tough chewin'.'

'You think he *ain't*? So far he's taken two of us out an' we ain't even set eyes on him yet.'

'You with me or agin' me?' growled Mark.

'Way I see it, I ain't got a choice,' replied Farrier. 'We all helped kill his damned nag so whether we stay together or not ain't gonna make any difference, except that together we stand a better chance of nailing the bastard.'

Farrier paused and glanced hurriedly around. 'The cow-son could be watchin' us right now,' he muttered. 'Something or somebody had to be holding Bret up there until just the right time.'

The two men dived in opposite directions, hunting concealment in the bushes.

There was no smile on Jeff's face as he quietly began to move away from the immediate vicinity. His feet slipped on some loose shale sending a shower of small stones into the valley.

Instantly the two men below began to spread a volley of shots into the face of the cliff knowing it would take a lot of luck using handguns to make a hit.

Jeff heard the pound of feet across the valley floor. The men knew his general position now and he could hear their cursing as they scrabbled up the side of the cliff, loosing off sporadic shots as they climbed in the hope of a lucky hit.

As it was, some bullets came close, whining and screaming as they ricocheted off nearby boulders. One was close enough to twitch the side of his jacket.

The bullets were getting too close for comfort so Jeff quickly cut away at a tangent to keep out of the line of fire as he gradually left his pursuers further and further behind.

As soon as he could no longer hear the noise of their progress, Jeff began to cut back down the cliff again. He needed a replacement mount and fast.

Once he reached the valley he ghosted through the trees to the trail in front of the cave where the two men had left the horses. Leading them quietly away he took them to where he had hidden his saddle gear and the packs. Quickly he threw his saddle on the big roman-nosed roan. The horse belonged to Farrier and Jeff had singled it out as the best of the bunch of four some time ago. Next he turned his attention to the pack-horse.

He had just finished strapping the packs in place when he heard movement in the trees. He ducked instinctively as a bee-like buzz followed by the sound of the shot warned him of his danger.

Ignoring the pack-horse he vaulted into the saddle and drove the big ugly roan directly towards the gunfire.

The two men had expected him to run in the opposite direction, away from the shooting. The sight of the big horse charging towards them was disconcerting, putting off their aim as they jumped aside to avoid the charging animal.

Jeff had no time to think of gun-play himself, he had all he could do to control the powerful horse.

Lying flat along its back to avoid low branches and make himself as small a target as possible, horse and rider raced between the trees to safety as the two cursing men sent futile bullets in search of him.

Jeff allowed the horse to have its head while it was pounding through the trees but as soon as he reached a wide trail he turned into it and gradually curbed the roan down to a canter.

He'd intended to collect all the horses and leave the two men afoot. He patted the neck of his new mount. 'Well, hoss, can't have everything,' he muttered. 'At least I got me a good hoss to ride even if I do have to go without grub for a while.'

Jeff rode for an hour before turning

off the trail and into the trees once again.

'Best get some shut-eye,' he muttered, as he dismounted and ground-hitched the roan.

Jeff left his saddle and bridle on the horse in case he had to move in a hurry.

Untying his bedroll from behind his saddle and slipping his Winchester from its boot he made a cold camp and was soon asleep.

8

Jeff was in the saddle as the false dawn slowly changed the night sky from indigo to pink and back again before the sun began to heave itself into the heavens chasing the darkness from the forest.

He kept the horse down to a walk as he began to ride over his back trail towards the cave. The birds were chirping and flitting through the trees in the cool of the early morning, but the awakening forest went unnoticed as Jeff tuned his senses to seek out other sounds, man-made noises which did not belong there.

It was past noon by the time Jeff had reconnoitred the area around the cave. He approached the opening, his senses tuned to pick up the slightest foreign sound, but there was nothing.

When he finally entered he discovered the body of Bret Keever. The two men had merely dragged him into the cave and had thrown a few rocks over him. Jeff's nose twitched in disgust at the smell that was beginning to permeate the cave. 'So much for brotherly love,' he muttered as he walked over to the fireplace he had made, and tested the ashes.

There was still a slight warmth there and he estimated that Keever and Farrier had eaten in the cave last night. He allowed the tension to ease out of his body. If they hadn't eaten here this morning it was a fair bet that they had left the cave after their meal the night before. They would hardly have slept here overnight and then left without even making coffee, he reasoned.

Jeff left the cave and began searching for tracks. It was good to get out of the sickly sweet smell of the cave and its contents, back into the warmth of the sunshine.

After an hour of painstaking search, Jeff could only conclude that the two had left the area.

He'd found where the horses had been picketed, the signs telling him that the animals had not been there for too long.

Jeff swung into the saddle and continued to follow the cleared trail leading through the forest. It was not possible to discover actual tracks since it was a regularly used game trail and any spoor would be quickly blended with those of wild animals.

Jeff rode on slowly, eyes always searching for any danger the forest might hold. The patience taught him by his Indian friends would not allow him to hurry.

Then he saw the horse droppings.

He smiled, his lips pulled into a thin, tight line. He knew he would find it eventually. A horse was bound to leave its calling card sooner or later. An Indian would remove it, or even place it somewhere else to confuse any pursuit but a white man would never even think of it.

Jeff slid from the saddle; the droppings were cold. He sat back on his haunches considering the possibilities.

The two had ridden this way last night after dumping brother Bret in the cave and eating a meal.

Jeff's saliva began to work at the thought of a meal.

All the signs indicated that the two men had decided to give up the chase and were heading out.

He threw away the short piece of stick he had been twirling in his hands, stood up and dusted off his jeans.

They might have given up, he thought grimly, but he hadn't.

The palomino had been more than a horse. Over the years it had become a friend. The only link with his past. The two men somewhere ahead had wantonly destroyed it so they had to pay.

There was nothing to consider. To the young man with the scar on his forehead it was as inevitable as night follows day; the fact that the two men seemed to be heading back to the town of Boswell where the diligent bartender would recognize him and a posse might still be ready to capture him made no difference at all.

He strolled over to the horse and mounted. 'At least I kin get some grub now I know those varmints are no longer around,' he told the horse. 'I'll just find me a cottontail an we'll be on our way. I hope them *hombres* give Boswell a miss but it sure don't look like it.'

He touched spurs to the horse. 'Let's git dinner,' he muttered.

9

It was nearing four o'clock when Jeff rode the big roman-nosed roan down the main street of Boswell.

Unlike the last time he'd been there, the sun was scorching the ground and dust devils whirled along as the horse's hooves disturbed it but nothing else seemed to be moving on the street as he pulled in at the hitching rail in front of the saloon.

Jeff slid tiredly from the saddle, tying the horse to the rail. He eased his guns in their holsters and pushed open the batwings.

The saloon was almost empty and, as he approached the bar, the same barkeep hurried to serve him, wiping his hands on a towel as he approached, a big friendly grin on his bewhiskered features.

'Hi, friend,' he called cheerfully.

'What'll it be? Whiskey? Beer? You name it we got it . . . say, don't I know you from somewhere?'

'We've already done that bit once, mister,' growled Jeff. 'It cost me a long ride an' a good horse.'

The barkeep stared harder. 'Say ain't you the . . . '

'Yeah,' agreed Jeff. 'The very same, an' if I get any more nonsense outa you I'm gonna get mighty upset, *comprende amigo?*'

'S-sure,' stuttered the barman. 'Hey I didn't mean . . . '

'Sure you did,' Jeff interrupted, being deliberately surly. 'An' if I remember right I left a full glass around here somewhere, I'll take it now if it's all the same to you.'

Sweat was oozing out of the barman's bald head and running down his nose. 'Yessir, one root beer comin' up,' he mumbled.

'Seen anything of Sheriff Keever or his pal Farrier?' Jeff asked quietly.

'Yeah,' replied the barman, eager to

please. 'They rode in a few days ago. Only Keever ain't sheriff no more; we got a new man in town now. He seems tough but fair. I reckon I've seen him before somewhere.'

'Don't you always!' grunted Jeff succinctly.

'Uh, yeah I do, don't I,' replied the barman. 'See you're ridin' Farrier's bronc.'

'Nosy sort of galoot, ain't you?'

'Um, no!' gulped the barman. 'It's just that Farrier let it be known that he'd had it stole by some thievin' . . . er I, that is . . . God, me an' my big mouth!' He swallowed painfully as he looked down the business end of Jeff's Colt.

'Nobody calls me a hossthief,' growled Jeff, keeping up his act. 'That Farrier *hombre* shot mine so I took his, an' *I* lost on the deal. Now, seeing as you're so God-damned nosy you can probably tell me just where I can find Keever and his buddy. If you can I just might forget that you cost me my bronc.'

'Yeah, yeah, ain't no secret, they're staying at the hotel down the road. Said they'd come back fer their pay but Mister Potter said as how they could whistle for it. Turned out to be a real he-man that one. Nobody don't poke fun at him any more I can tell you.'

Jeff finished his beer and wiped his mouth. 'I'm going out now,' he said quietly, 'an' before you go chasing off to this new sheriff to tell him I'm in town, don't bother! In the first place that dodger is out of date an' in the second, I intend to tell him that myself, d'you understand?'

'Oh sure sure, you ain't wanted an' I should take the notice down, right!'

'Right!' agreed Jeff as he turned from the bar and walked into the main street.

He stopped and looked back over the batwings. 'You sure we understand each other, mister?' he growled, in a deliberately threatening voice.

'Y'yes sir, mister,' mumbled the barkeep. 'I sure do understand you, clear as daylight I surely do.'

Jeff touched the front of his J.B. in a quick salute, 'Just make sure you remember,' he growled, as he turned and walked away.

He was strolling slowly down the road when he saw a tall man ease out of the doorway of the sheriff's office.

He just seemed to curl around the door post and lounge there as if he had no place to go and wasn't in a hurry to get there. He looked about as peaceful as a coiled diamond-back and twice as dangerous.

Jeff didn't pause in his slow progress; to all outward signs he too was half asleep as he studied the man from under the brim of his soiled stetson.

The man was well dressed, with a grey ten gallon on his head. His shirt was a bright new checkered pattern, partly covered by an expensive-looking, grey, soft-leather vest. The pants too were clean and neat, the Levis clinging tightly to his spare frame tucked into well-polished, high-sided riding boots which were decorated with heavy Mexican star rowels. Jeff was surprised to see jinglebobs hanging from the spurs. They were very decorative but the jingle would give fair warning that he was around.

The twin Colt Navys were snugged into cutaway holsters and the *hombre* looked as if he knew where to find 'em in a hurry. The rifle held carelessly in one slack hand was the new 1866 Winchester repeating rifle.

Jeff was aware that the man lounging so indolently against the door post was giving him the same detailed scrutiny.

Guess I come out a poor second, Jeff thought sourly as he considered his own unkempt appearance.

He hadn't seen the inside of a bath in three months, and the way he was feeling, if he left it much longer he wouldn't have to ride a horse, the fleas would be able to carry him around without half trying.

As he passed the man he heard the

tinkle of the jinglebobs, their sound measuring the man's pace behind him.

The hotel where Keever and Farrier were supposed to be staying was directly ahead of him fronting the street.

He tensed as he saw Mike Farrier leave the place and walk slowly down the front steps of the boardwalk into the hard-packed road.

Dust devils, stirred by vagrant puffs of wind still lifted and fell on the grit and dust road and a tumbleweed came cavorting around the corner up there by the hotel.

Jeff realized that Farrier had seen him some time ago. The man stood legs apart, balanced as he gave his guns a tentative push to flare out the grips for a fast draw.

Jeff also eased his Colt Frontiers in their holsters without pausing in his easy progress. Dimly behind him he heard the tinkle of the jinglebobs and a cold knot settled in the pit of his stomach.

Farrier was slightly crouched, waiting, poised ready to slap leather. They were less than sixty feet apart and closing.

Jeff could take the man in front, he was sure of it, but he could never beat the rifle behind him.

The jinglebobs were still there as he cut the distance to forty feet.

'Let's just hold it right there!' The voice was cold, even, and deadly. 'First man tries to draw iron dies.'

The two combatants stared stonily at each other, neither willing to make the first move.

'This is private business mister, butt out and let's git it done,' growled Jeff.

'This is my bailiwick. In this town no shooting is private,' replied the man evenly. 'You want to kill each other do it outside the town limits.'

'He's a hossthief, mister,' shouted Farrier. 'That's my nag tied to the rail up there. Where I come from we used tuh hang hossthieves.'

'You ever see this feller before?' asked the voice.

'No, but that's my hoss right enough.'

'Could be he found it an' just brought it into town looking fer the owner. What say you, mister, that how it was?'

Jeff realized that the man was giving him a chance to back off from a showdown but that was not his way.

'No, that ain't how it was,' he replied evenly. 'The fella there helped shoot my horse so I took his. Like I said to the barkeep, I lost on the deal. Now, get off my back, mister, or face me up front like a man.'

'Easy now,' cautioned the voice. 'Nobody's facing nobody. Now, both of you, nice and slowly, put your hands behind your heads.'

The two men reluctantly complied. 'That's just jim-dandy,' continued the sheriff. 'Now you, fella, down by the hotel, walk up here. Keep it slow now and keep the hands behind the head.'

Realizing he had no alternative, Farrier reluctantly complied and continued to walk until he was standing beside Mason.

'Just hold it right there,' commanded the voice. 'Now you, mister, turn around.'

Jeff did as he was told. 'Right,' continued the sheriff. 'Both start walking towards my office, an' if either of you so much as thinks about reaching for iron, *don't*! Because I'll drop you so fast you won't even know you're dead, *sabe*?'

The two men marched slowly forward, Jeff could hear the jinglebobs timing out the man's measured pace behind them.

Jeff was surprised that there was no crowd on the street; it seemed that no one was even interested in what was happening and the road remained empty.

The doorway to the sheriff's office was a double one so there was plenty of room for the two men to enter side by side. The sheriff's heel caught in a broken piece of planking in the boardwalk as the two men entered the office, making him stumble slightly. It would not have mattered but the jinglebobs told the story.

Farrier turned, faster than a striking snake. Stepping in front of Mason he smashed his fist into the young man's groin. As Jeff doubled over in pain, Farrier's gun bored into his stomach so that he was using Jeff as a shield against the other man's rifle.

'Put it down. *Now!*' he snarled. 'Or I'll blow a hole in him big enough to run a wagon through.'

'Yeah? Well, just go ahead,' invited the sheriff. 'Second you do, you're dead also.'

Jeff was rapidly regaining his wind; he could sense the hesitation by the way Farrier's gun pressure was easing. Another few seconds and he'd be able to take a hand in the game.

Farrier must have realized the danger. Still keeping Jeff between himself and the rifle, he stepped backwards as he drew his second gun. He kept back-pedalling until he felt the desk behind him, then he stepped around it and crouched. He now had the bulk of the desk as protection.

He gave a little chuckle of exultation as he indicated towards the bars of the cells. 'Right, Mason, or whatever yuh call yourself, git over there.'

'Stay right where you are,' snapped the voice from outside.

Jeff sighed. 'If I stay here, mister, the guy in front of me is gonna shoot; if I move you're gonna shoot — that's one hell'uva choice to give a fella. But if I was a betting man I'd rather lay my money on you not shooting me in the back.'

'You'd be wrong,' growled the sheriff.

'I've bin wrong before,' replied Jeff with a shrug, as he moved towards the bars and out of the doorway.

'Hey, you out there,' called Mike Farrier. 'Why don't you-all come on in an pay a visit.'

'Any particular reason why I should,' answered the voice.

'Well you-all seemed kinda determined tuh stop us killing each other back there on the road,' he taunted. 'Could be I'll blow his damned head off and mess up your nice clean jail if you don't come in.'

'So go to it,' growled the sheriff. 'When it's over you still have to come out. No other way but through the front doors, an' I ain't got no place to go for a week or so.'

It looked as though there would be no break in the stalemate, but at that moment Roland Potter came bowling along completely oblivious to the fact that the man he, together with other responsible townsmen had appointed as temporary sheriff, was standing outside his own office holding a rifle.

'Ah, good day to you, Captain Malloy,' breezed Potter as he bowled merrily towards the doors of the sheriff's office. 'Come in, there's a good chap, some words in private if you would be so kind.'

Before Malloy could stop him Roland Potter was inside the office and cruising up to the desk.

He stopped dead at the sight of Mike Farrier leaning on the desk, pointing a gun at his ample mid-section.

Potter ignored the fact that the other gun seemed to be pointing towards the cells. He was only interested in the one looking his way.

He swallowed the sudden lump in his throat with obvious difficulty. 'Er um, Sheriff,' Potter called weakly. 'Did you, um, know there's a man in here with a gun pointing in my direction?'

'Yeah, I knew,' replied Malloy tiredly, realizing that his bargaining point had just disappeared.

'Do wish you'd have said,' mumbled Potter. Then, with a flash of bravery he snapped, 'Mister Farrier, will you please put that gun away, you are no longer deputy here, and I've already told you that you'll get no back pay from me.'

He looked over his shoulder and saw

Jeff Mason from the corner of his eye. He did a quick double take. 'M-my *goodness*, it's you isn't it!' he muttered disbelievingly. 'What in heaven's name are *you* doing in our sheriff's office?'

He turned as if to wander over to Jeff.

'Stand still Roly,' snapped Farrier. 'You're gonna be my way out of here.'

Before anyone could do anything Farrier slipped around from behind the desk and stuck his Colt into Potter's ample middle.

'Ow, that hurt,' grumbled Potter.

'Turn around,' snapped Farrier, keeping a wary eye on Mason. 'You an' me are takin' a walk as far as the hotel.' He raised his voice. 'You hear me out there? Me an' Potter's gonna stroll down to the hotel; he'll keep me company until I collect my duds then I'll be on my way.'

'What happens to Potter?'

'Nothin', unless you start something.'

'OK, come on out,' replied Malloy resignedly.

Farrier turned to Jeff with a grimace of hate. 'I'll see you again, feller.'

'You'd better pray you don't,' replied Jeff evenly as Mike Farrier pushed Roland Potter towards the doors.

'You can't hold me,' sneered Farrier as he passed the sheriff. 'You just ain't smart enough, mister.'

'Early days yet,' replied Malloy evenly. 'If you ain't gone by tomorrow I'll come a-lookin', an' you better be good with that iron, mister,' he called as Farrier, pushing Potter, hurried towards the hotel.

Malloy watched pensively as Farrier entered the hotel with the fat man as a prisoner, unaware that Jeff was now standing beside him.

'You should have left me to it,' grunted Jeff. 'Would have saved you a lot of trouble.'

'No trouble,' replied Malloy absently, still staring at the hotel.

'How come you was prepared to let that jasper plug me, but the moment old Potter rolled up you backed down?'

'Mister Potter's a town councillor, you're just a drifter,' replied Malloy. 'He dies, the town would be crawling all over me; you die; so who cares!'

'Oh that's *very* nice. So what happened to civic rights?' Jeff stepped closer to Malloy as he spoke.

Malloy wrinkled his nose. 'D'you mind standing downwind, feller, you smell kinda ripe.'

'I feel kinda ripe, but that don't mean you can write me off just like that. Come to that I ain't exactly fond of you either.'

'Tell you what, why don't you mosey on down to the barber shop, have a good soak, change your duds, then come back here; I'll maybe buy you a beer an' we can have a friendly chat.'

'That's easy to say, feller. They give credit at this here barbershop? 'Cos my pockets is so empty even the moths have given up on me.'

'With that kind of smell dogging your tail like an over-friendly puppy I ain't surprised,' replied Malloy. 'Why the hell do I get all the drifters?'

He slipped a hand into his pocket and produced some money. He selected three silver cartwheels and offered them to Jeff. 'You go git your damned bath an' some grub; maybe I'll have a proposition that will interest you later.'

Jeff looked at the three dollars doubtfully, he hadn't been brought up to take hand-outs.

'G'wan take it,' urged Malloy, seeing his hesitation. 'You can pay me back sometime. Anyway, I figger I'm doing the town a favour, that stink can't be good for an up and comin' place like Boswell, an' if you-all keep them fleas on you much longer they'll steal more than three dollars' worth of meat off the people hereabouts.'

Jeff grinned self-consciously as he reluctantly took the money. 'OK you've convinced me. Maybe I don't dislike you as much as I thought. Point me towards the barbershop an' I'll do the town a favour.'

Malloy jerked his thumb over his

shoulder. 'It's back thataway. Better put that bronc out of sight too while you're at it, unless you want it stole back again.'

'Yeah, thanks,' replied Jeff, as he moved away. He paused. 'Ain't no business of mine but them jinglebobs is a dead give-away if you were stalking somethin'.'

'Ever hear of moccasins? Anyway, sometimes it pays to let a body know you're around, makes 'em kinda cautious if they know someone's behind 'em — saves on cartridges,' grunted Malloy.

A knowing grin spread across Jeff's face, the *hombre* was every bit as smart as he'd first thought.

He waved a hand. 'See you later,' he called as he headed for the barbershop.

10

Dusk was beginning to pull its shadows over the tiny township as Jeff entered the sheriff's office. Malloy was in the process of trimming the wick of the oil lamp.

He looked up at the sound of footsteps, his face pulling into a lop-sided grin as he recognized his visitor.

'Waal now,' he grunted. 'You sure smell sweeter. Bin using that there bath oil old Josh keeps fer the bankers and such?'

'Yeah.' Jeff grinned self-consciously. 'Sure smells sweet, don't it?'

'*Sweet!*' ejaculated Malloy in mock disgust. 'You smell like half a dozen whores in a very small room. If I take you down to the saloon smelling like that we'll have a riot on our hands.'

'Strong, huh?'

'*Strong!* Sonny, I reckon a Pawnee

with a head cold would smell you comin' three days' ride away.'

'That strong, huh?'

'Yep, an' I gotta admit the smell don't fit those God-awful duds; look like hand-me-downs from an out-of-work scarecrow.'

Jeff looked down sorrowfully at his very torn and dirty jacket. His jeans left a bit to be desired too, mired in dried mud and ripped by trees in his encounter back there in the woods. His run-over riding boots looked a mess too; one of them had the beginnings of a split down one side.

Jeff fingered the red bandanna turned tightly around his neck.

'Guess I don't exactly look the part of the most prosperous man in the world,' he grunted. 'Once I get me a riding job I'll soon put that right. But there's one thing I wanna git straight right now.'

Jeff walked over to the big notice-board and pointed at one of the dodgers.

'That's me! An' I have to tell you that I ain't no bank robber nor thief either . . . '

'I know,' Malloy cut in.

Jeff turned and stared at Malloy. 'You *know*?'

'Yep, you're Jeff Mason, a young cowpoke whose folks were killed by the Kincaid gang. I know all about you, son, an' I know how good you are with those guns too. I bin hoping to meet up with you but I didn't lay much on my chances. Knew it was you though, minute I set eyes on you, on account of the red bandanna.'

Jeff touched it subconsciously. 'You seem to know an awful lot about me, mister; seems to me this town is plumb full of people minding other folks' business.'

'Yeah, ain't that the truth?' replied Malloy. 'I also know you only wear it to cover a rope scar you got when you was almost hanged.'

Jeff stared at the sheriff; he was beginning to wonder about this hairpin, and he was also beginning to feel a tingle of irritation. 'Quite a little mine of information ain't yuh, mister?' he growled. 'I owe you three dollars but that don't keep my temper even forever.'

Malloy laughed. 'Don't get so all-fired het up, fella, I want us to be friends, especially since I got most of this information from a mutual friend anyway.'

'Friend? Didn't know I had any.'

'You're forgetting Nathaniel Kyle? You did him one hell of a favour a couple of years ago,' replied Malloy, still grinning.

'*Nathan*! You mean you know him? Last I heard he was heading for Casa Verde, he was gonna tell the law that I'm innocent, I never stole anything in my life.'

'Oh, he did that right enough, but he didn't stay there, couldn't wait to git back to Texas where his roots were. Fact is he lives about six miles out of town.'

'*This* town!'

'Yup; said if I should ever meet up with you I should tell you there's an open invite waiting should you ever want to take it up.'

'Well *hot damn*,' ejaculated Jeff. 'I'm sure gonna ride out there and see the old son-of-a-gun! How's Sarah?'

'Oh she's real fine, so's the youngster.'

'No kidding! A yearling huh?'

'Yup. Young Jeff's doing just fine, real hellion he is, reckon he'll be riding bucking broncos before he's two.'

Jeff felt a constriction in his throat. 'Called him Jeff, huh?'

He was remembering how it had been just over two years ago in the Dakotas. 'Guess I'll take me a ride out there tomorrow,' he muttered.

'Not in them duds you don't,' growled Malloy, with false anger. 'They're real friends of mine an' I ain't taking no scarecrow out to meet my godson, no sir. We'll git you set up with some proper duds tomorrow an' ride out together.'

'You forget, I'm broke.'

'Money ain't a problem, son,' replied Malloy. 'Nathaniel set some of the reward money aside in case you ever needed it; he's gonna be as pleased as punch to be able to give it to you, so stop worrying.'

'We've still got to deal with Mike Farrier, or have you forgotten he's holding Mister Potter prisoner?'

'Where do you get the *we* from? I'm the sheriff here, even if it is only acting sheriff until the town dignitaries get a permanent one. I'll just mosey on down to the hotel an' collect the fat man. I don't think for one minute Farrier is gonna get his name on a dodger if he can avoid it so you go and find a place to get some sleep and meet me here in the morning OK?'

'What about that beer?'

'With you smelling like that? Believe me, I got more sense. See you around.'

He gave Jeff a careless wave as he started towards the hotel, the tinkle of the jinglebobs telling all and sundry that the sheriff was on the street.

Even with the cost of stabling and feeding the roan and himself Jeff still had more than enough of the three dollars left to get himself a room, but as he'd already been told by the hostler that the hotel down the road was the only one in town, he decided to go back to the stable and sleep close to his new mount. He didn't want to cramp the sheriff's style, nor did he want to lose the horse.

He felt considerably better after having a haircut and filling his belly properly for the first time in weeks. So, after negotiating with the hostler for a spare stall close to his mount he spread out his bedroll. Using his saddle for a pillow he very quickly dropped into a deep sleep.

11

Jeff was leaning against the door of the sheriff's office when he heard the tinkle of the jinglebobs approaching through the gloom of the early morning.

Sheriff Malloy touched the brim of his stetson as he approached. 'Mornin' Mason,' he grunted.

'Well it *was*,' replied Jeff, with a hint of sarcasm. 'You should have told me you don't get to work till midday.'

'Oh *God!*' muttered the sheriff, sniffing the air.

'Aw come on,' answered Jeff with a grin. 'Don't tell me you can still smell that stuff.'

'That was plenty bad enough, but mixed with the smell of hoss manure an' stables — Holy Jesus. You sure ain't no ladies' man, I can tell that right off. I think we'd better git you fixed up with some new duds, another bath and some grub before I take you out to the Kyle place. Smelling like you do right now I reckon you'll be about as welcome as a polecat at a picnic. Come on.'

Jeff ambled along beside his new-found friend, content to see what the day held in store. He was looking forward to meeting Nathan and Sarah Kyle again and it showed.

'You look like a kid who's been given a jar of sweets,' chuckled Malloy.

'Kinda feel like it too,' replied Jeff. 'Say, what do I call you, I can't just call you Sheriff, can I?'

'Ma used to call me Luke; you can use that if it suits.'

'Yeah, fine. I'm kinda glad I met up with you, Luke, but I heard Mister Potter call you Captain, were you in the war?'

'Wasn't everybody?'

'I wasn't; apart from being too young at the time I was brought up on an isolated little ranch in Indian territory, didn't even know about the war until I met Nathan. You were a captain, huh?'

'Yep, still am, in the Texas Rangers. We're re-forming. Tell you about it on the ride out to Nathan's place, meantime let's get you fixed up decent.'

'I get to pay you back though,' replied Jeff.

'Bet your sweet life you do, son,' grunted Luke, 'I don't do hand-outs to tramps, not even friendly ones, especially when they stink to high heaven.'

'How did you manage last night collecting Mister Potter? I mean, did you get any trouble from Farrier or Keever?' asked Jeff, as they entered the store.

'No, it was like I said, just a bluff to get out of a tight spot. Matter of fact, I met Potter coming out of the hotel, he was mad enough to chew iron and spit nails. Told me the two *hombres* had already split the breeze. Don't think we'll be hearin' from them in a hurry.'

Malloy looked at the proprietor of the store who was waiting with a questioning look on his face. 'Hi, Henry,' he grinned. 'I'm about to make your day. Take a long look at the scarecrow standing beside me.'

Henry, a tall lean man with mutton-chop whiskers, rubbed his hands as he looked Jeff up and down speculatively. His nose twitched as he caught the blend of smells.

'Well, what's he gonna need to make him look respectable?' asked Malloy.

'Yuh mean apart from a bath?'

'Yeah,' grinned Malloy.

'Just about a new everything I reckon, 'cept guns,' replied Henry, a predatory grin spreading across his face as he rubbed his bony hands together in anticipation. 'But he don't look as if he's got change fer ten cents, an' I don't give credit to drifters. 'Course looks kin be deceivin'; you don't happen to be one of them eccentric millionaires do yuh, mister?'

'Nope he ain't,' answered Malloy before Jeff could think of a suitable reply. 'Just you put it on Nathaniel Kyle's tab, an' if he don't settle I will; that suit yuh Henry?'

'Good as gold in the bank,' replied Henry, as he went to work with a will.

'Sort yourself out a good set of duds, top to bottom,' Malloy told Jeff. 'Then for God's sake take a bath *before* you put 'em on. I'm gonna get me some breakfast. I'll expect you at the office around ten o'clock and we'll ride out to Nathan's place. Oh, and one other small thing, don't use any of that stinking lotion in the bath water, OK?'

Jeff grinned. 'Learning, learning, all the time learning. See you at ten. So long Luke, and thanks.'

'Don't thank me,' grinned Luke, as he walked away. 'Nathan will be glad to pay out of the reward money, fella.'

It was way past noon as Jeff Mason and Luke Malloy rode over the ridge and directed their mounts towards the small homestead nestling in the valley.

The tall, rawboned man heading towards the house was not hard to recognize. He paused as he caught sight of two riders, and raised a hand to shield his eyes against the sun.

Jeff waved and he saw the big man straighten up, his body tense. Jeff removed his brand new stetson and waved it as he kicked the roan into a fast trot, giving a shrill cowboy yell.

The reply was instant, the *Yahoo* echoed across the valley in welcome.

It took but a few moments for the tiny, white-aproned form of Sarah to appear in the doorway to see what all the commotion was about.

Always wary, Jeff noticed, as he entered the yard in a swirl of dust, Sarah had not forgotten to tote along the 30.30 he remembered so well.

Although Jeff had filled out a great deal over the past two years, he felt like a kid again as Nathan grabbed him around the waist and hauled him off his feet, swinging him around like a yearling and damn near crushing his ribs in the process.

'God-damn but it's real good to see you Jeff,' Nathan shouted, grinning from ear to ear. 'We bin lookin' at that rise ever since we settled here hoping to see you ride over the brow; last we heard you was riding the Bozeman Trail with a herd of steers heading for Montana.'

All the time he had been talking, Nathan had been holding Jeff in a bone-crushing grip, and Jeff's feet were still some six inches off the ground.

'Put him down, you great bear, an' let me get my hug in,' snapped his wife, with false anger.

Jeff was thankful when Nathan released him to make way for Sarah, who could hardly wait to get her arms around him; then it was Jeff's turn to lift her off her feet while he hugged her.

After a few moments he held her off while he studied the tiny but resolute woman who had saved not only his own life, but Nathan's too.

The worry-lines had smoothed out of her face leaving her looking years younger than when he had last seen her.

She was as smart and trim as ever in her gingham dress and spotless white apron, but more than anything Jeff noticed the tranquillity in her eyes. 'Is life treating you right, Sarah?' he asked in quiet sincerity.

'Better than right, Jeff,' she smiled, as she flicked a rebellious tear from her eyes. 'And this is the icing on the cake. Seeing you again makes everything just perfect. D'you know we've got a son? Are you staying for good? Don't let Captain Malloy talk you into anything . . . '

'Whoah, ease up there, Sarah,' Jeff laughingly interrupted the tirade. 'You're making more noise than a Pawnee in a rain dance. God-damn but it's good to see you all . . . '

'Don't blaspheme,' Sarah interrupted in her turn. 'You're slipping into ungodly ways, Jeff Mason, and I won't have it, you hear?'

'Yes ma'am,' replied Jeff meekly as they linked arms and went into the neat little farmhouse to see the new baby, while Nathan and Luke Malloy trailed behind them, both eager to see Jeff's reaction to the new offspring.

12

Mark Keever and Mike Farrier had ridden away from town as quickly as possible; they had no wish to test the wrath of Luke Malloy and Mason. Together they would make a formidable pair.

Keever was still hoping to get even for the death of his brother, and Mike Farrier wanted his horse, or at least one as good, before he left the territory.

It was sheer chance that they chose to ride westward out of town, directly towards the farmstead of Nathaniel and Sarah Kyle.

They were resting in a small copse some three miles out of town when they heard the clop of horses' hooves passing nearby.

Keever grabbed the two horses and held their muzzles to stop them from betraying their presence while his partner slipped quietly through the trees to see who the riders were.

Mike Farrier silently cursed his luck. If he'd thought to bring his rifle he could have blown Mason and Malloy from the saddle from the safety of the trees, but he only had his pistols and the two riders were too far away to try taking them out with sidearms.

Farrier watched as they gradually passed over a slight rise and rode on out of sight. 'They ain't huntin' us that's fer sure,' he muttered. 'But with both of 'em headin' out of town, could be we should head back.'

Quickly he slipped back to where Keever was waiting for him, Keever's eyes asking the question.

'No sweat,' grunted Farrier. 'Mason an' Malloy riding out somewheres I guess.'

'On *your* hoss?' sneered Keever.

'Yep,' replied Farrier, with a sly smile. 'But that leaves the town kinda short on law. Malloy ain't even appointed a deputy yet, nor a town marshal either.'

'You ain't thinking of the bank!'

'Why the hell not?' replied Farrier. 'You know as well as I do we're both on Wanted posters, an' it'll only be a matter of time before we'll see our mugs plastered in towns all over Texas. I reckon Malloy is a Ranger anyhow.'

'Yeah, could be,' replied Keever thoughtfully. 'But we'd be a bit short-handed with just the two of us; pity young Bret got hisself hanged by that Mason *hombre*. Three's just right. Two inside an' one watchin' the hosses. You sure Malloy an' his side-kick is heading out?'

'Plumb certain,' replied Farrier, as they swung into their kaks and kicked their mounts into a canter. 'Say, what about that greaser, Sanchos? He was supposed to show up in town today to see if we'd punched Mason's ticket, reckon he might go for a third share?'

'Could be,' grunted Keever. 'Seems the kind of *hombre* who'd be willing to make a fast dollar. Reckon he'd be good with that machete in a pinch. He could hold the hosses for us while we do the business. What happens to him after we get clear would be another thing altogether.' He finished with a wolfish smile.

'Yeah,' grinned his companion. 'It could finish up with a two-way split come sundown. Sure wish I had my own hoss under me, though.'

'Yeah,' sneered Keever. 'Careless that, losing a hoss is a bad business. Should have remembered where you put it.' He kicked his mount into a fast gallop before Farrier could give his blistering reply.

The town seemed quiet as they rode down the main street some twenty minutes later.

They had slowed to a steady walk for the last two miles to make sure their horses were in fine fettle should a mad dash be called for.

The midday sun was blistering down and the horses sent up dust devils as they plodded down the street.

There were a few poke-bonneted women going about their business with shopping baskets on their arms. Two old-timers sat in rockers with their stained stetsons tilted over their eyes, feet pushing against the hitching rail by the sheriff's office.

'Nothing to get excited about,' muttered Keever from the corner of his mouth. 'Reckon we might pick up old Potter from his office as a hostage afore we go in.'

'Yeah, good idea, we owe him one anyway,' replied his companion, as he tilted his hat over his eyes and slouched in apparent indolence. The eyes under the hat were gimlet sharp, however, as they flickered from one place to another.

'By the dry-goods store,' he grunted, as he spotted what looked to be a bundle of rags heaped in a shaded corner covered by a large serape and topped with a disreputable-looking sombrero.

The bundle moved slightly as the

sombrero tilted enough to allow Sanchos Alvarez to see who was riding down the street. Then, the bundle straightened and slipped quickly down the narrow passage between the dry-goods store and the livery.

With casual ease the two riders turned their mounts into the alley and followed.

The Mexican was waiting in heavy shadow halfway down the alley and the two men dismounted beside him.

'Well, *señors*, do you bring me the news I hope for?'

'Nope, he got away, killed my brother too,' grunted Keever in disgust. 'Fact is he was in town until this mornin'.'

Sanchos seemed to shrink as he crossed himself. '*Si*, I am not surprised, he has come for me. Wherever I go, El Lobo Diablo will follow me, he cannot be killed.'

Mark Keever chuckled disbelievingly. 'Say, this Mason hairpin has really got to you, huh. What makes you think he can't be killed?'

'*Por favor, señors* but you do not know. I myself have killed him twice. Once here.' He placed a hand on his heart. 'And once here.' Sanchos placed a finger on his forehead. 'Yet still he haunts me. Now I must leave as fast as I can.' He shrugged in hopeless resignation. 'But still he will find me one day.'

Keever sobered a little at the tale. 'I gotta admit the Jasper sure takes some killin', but somebody'll write his ticket sooner or later.'

'*Si*, I suppose so,' replied Sanchos without much conviction, 'but when, eh?'

'Never mind all that,' Farrier interrupted. 'We're gonna hit the bank while the sheriff's out of town but we need an extra hand to hold the broncs. We can be in and out in less than ten minutes. Figgered you might be interested in picking up some quick dinero, how's about it?'

Avarice flashed across the Mexican's face at the thought, fighting the fear that had burrowed deep into his brain.

Avarice won . . . just! 'How much do you think is in there, and what will be my share?' he asked cautiously.

'Straight three-way split,' replied Farrier, giving his partner a knowing look.

'*Si*, I'm in,' replied the Mexican, his innate greed stifling his fears of the man he called El Lobo Diablo. I will get my *caballo, un momento, señors.*'

Sanchos scurried to the rear end of the alley and returned in a few moments leading a powerful-looking skewbald stallion.

'You were all ready for a fast get-away, huh, Sanchos?' grunted Farrier, impressed in spite of his low opinion of anyone not white. 'That's some bronc you have feller,' he continued, already making up his mind that the horse would more than replace the one he'd had stolen by Mason.

'*Si, señor,*' replied Sanchos. 'It is always a good thing for a Mexican to have a good *caballo* when he is in a white man's town; once I cross the border into Mexico things will be different.'

'They sure will,' Keever replied, grinning slyly at his partner as the trio mounted and drifted easily back into the sun-scorched street and made their slow way towards the bank.

The street remained reassuringly empty until they reached the assay office close to the bank. Then, Roland Potter and Brad Peters came out of the assay office chatting together.

'Must be our lucky day, two for the price of one,' grunted Mark Keever as he nodded to the two men.

'Yup,' replied Farrier succinctly, as he slowed his mount to keep pace with the two pedestrians.

'You ready, greaser?' grunted Keever disparagingly as slowly they all approached the doors of the bank.

'*Si*,' muttered Sanchos, showing his dislike at the slur.

Keever and Farrier slid from their saddles in one easy movement, without allowing the horses to break their leisurely pace.

Guns slid into ready hands as they stepped behind the two townsmen while Sanchos leaned across and collected the reins of the two horses, easing them to a halt beside the hitching rail.

Roland Potter and his friend had no sense of impending danger until the sixguns bored into their backs.

'Just keep the hands down an' keep walking natural like,' growled Keever in threatening undertones, as the two gunmen propelled their captives along under the pressure of their guns.

Roland Potter was getting a bit fed up with having guns pushed into him. 'If this is your idea of a joke, Keever,' he said rather pompously, 'I would advise you to put the gun away, climb on your mount and ride out of town while you still have the chance, because . . . '

'Shut your stupid, fat mouth,' snarled Keever. 'You haven't got half the town around you now, and Malloy has gone riding with the Mason hairpin. So, unless you want all that wind let out through holes in your fat carcass you'll do as I say. In here,' he continued as they turned the two men towards the doors of the bank. 'We need to take out a few pesos to tide us over like.'

Before either of the two townsmen could protest they were propelled into the bank and pushed up to the counter where a middle-aged teller with tired, rather sombre features stared listlessly from behind the protective grille in the otherwise empty bank.

'Afternoon Mister Potter, Mister Peters,' he singsonged uninterestedly as he had done for the last twenty years of working behind various bank grilles. 'What can we do for you this fine day?'

Suddenly the teller became interested as the muzzle of a Colt .45 poked through the grille right under his nose, and he desperately tried to swallow the sudden lump in his throat.

'Call the manager over,' grunted Keever. 'No, don't turn around.' He spoke sharply as the frightened man attempted to leave his seat. 'Just call him over, quiet like.'

The man seemed to have difficulty in articulating, he made two more attempts to swallow the lump in his throat before he managed to croak, 'Mister Priest sir, c-could you come over here a moment please?'

The manager, a florid-faced individual, looked up from his accounting sheets, recognized two of his most important customers and pushed his heavy bulk away from the desk with a wide welcoming smile on his face, the rather flamboyant vest straining at the seams as the man stretched his arms sideways in an effort to ease his cramped muscles as he approached the grilled window.

'Good afternoon gentlemen,' he almost purred. 'What can we do today for our two most prominent citizens?'

The genial smile froze as he saw the gun and his bulk seemed to shrink.

'Nice of you to ask,' grunted Farrier.

'D'you happen to have a nice big burlap sack handy?'

'Er, well, yes I do as it happens,' replied Priest hesitantly.

'Good,' responded Farrier, 'just get it and fill it up.' Mike Farrier pulled the hammer back to full cock, the sound loud in the stillness of the bank.

'Now look here,' Priest exploded in sudden anger. 'This is everything I own; if you clean out this bank I'm ruined!'

'Which way do you want it, ruined or dead?' snarled Keever, getting a little jittery at the delay. 'Now, move it before we lose our patience.'

George Priest glanced desperately at Potter and his friend, as if silently asking what he should do.

Potter shrugged, interpreting the look. 'Better do as they say, George, seems like they've changed from lawmen to law-breakers in one easy step. Maybe they'll learn their manners when Luke Malloy returns, especially if he brings that Mason hellion back with him.'

The sixgun gouged into his back making him wince. 'Just keep the lip buttoned, fat boy, or you won't get to use it again,' growled Farrier. 'An' you, George, git that bag an' fill it as fast as you can otherwise there'll be a lot of dead men in here, *comprende*?'

George Priest had spent most of his life in banking working for other people. He'd saved, bought and sold until he had reached the height of his ambitions, owning his very own bank. Yet in moments it would all be gone. He heaved a sigh of defeat as he slowly collected a bag from under the counter, walked to the safe and opened it.

He turned hopefully as the doors clattered open, but it was only two women chattering away about the weather, closely followed by Sanchos. The tableau held for a few moments as everyone eyed each other.

The two women backed instinctively towards the doors only to be stopped by Sanchos who had a revolver in one hand and his machete in the other.

Roland Potter was one of the last to turn, then he stiffened. '*Rosamund*,' he blurted without thought.

Keever grinned evilly. 'Li'l wife come to put her hard-earned dollars in the bank fer us has she? Now I think that's very nice of her.' He waved the Colt at her. 'Come right on over, *Rosamund*,' he leered. 'Just you put that there money-bag right here on the counter.'

The teller had been gradually easing his hand around the grip of a double-action Tranter he kept under the counter for just such an emergency. It would cut clean through the thin planking in front of him.

His only problem was that he could not be sure just where the gun was pointing. He hoped it was towards Keever who was standing away from his hostage while he was baiting Potter's wife.

The teller was no gunman; he just pulled the trigger and hoped that in the confusion, the banker or one of the others would take the initiative and do

132

something to prevent the robbery.

The bullet smashed through the planking, flattening as it did so. It punched a hole the size of a dollar in Mrs Potter's left breast and slapped the woman down as if she'd run into a train.

Potter screamed, '*ROSAMUND!*' as he pushed Mike Farrier aside with almost contemptuous ease and charged towards his fallen wife.

George Priest saw his chance and grabbed for the Colt he always kept in the safe.

He was turning, bringing up the gun when Farrier regained his balance.

The two men faced each other for a second but Farrier's reflexes were more finely turned than the banker's.

His first bullet bored into Priest's shoulder deflecting the banker's aim. The second took him just above the heart. He was dead before he hit the floor, but he still managed to pull the trigger. Brad Peters died with the bullet through his throat.

The teller, his eyes still tightly closed, fired a second shot through the planking cutting a groove along Keever's side. Keever spun on his heels and fanned two quick shots through the teller's grille.

The force of the bullets lifted the teller from his seat and dumped him on the top of his dead employer.

Sanchos had not fired a shot. He began to ease towards the door as he heard shouts from outside as the townsfolk were roused by the shooting.

Keever and Farrier looked at each other trying to decide whether to go for the money or run.

The noise was getting louder so, by mutual consent, they dashed after the disappearing Sanchos.

The three hit the saddles as one. The Mexican's mount shot into the lead as bullets began to buzz around the fleeing men like angry hornets.

A man rushed into the road waving a gun, only to be brushed aside by the Mexican's mount. Sanchos made no move to fire, leaning low along his mount's neck making himself as small a target as possible, riding as if the Devil himself were on his heels, and to Sanchos he was. A devil he had named El Lobo was always there, just a few paces behind him.

Keever and Farrier fired right and left, bearing a charmed life as they rode down the main street towards open country and freedom.

A man was running down the street carrying a double-barrelled shot-gun. Sanchos had already passed him but Keever and his sidekick were coming up fast.

The shot-gun came up but both horsemen fired together, their bullets slapping the man into the dust before he'd even had chance to depress the triggers.

Never again would the barkeep with the bald head and heavy side whiskers say, 'What'll it be?' or, 'Say! don't I know you from somewhere?'

The three men cleared town

unscathed but penniless, knowing it would not take long for the townsmen to organize a posse and begin searching for them.

They also knew that once Luke Malloy returned to town the search would start in earnest; he was not the type to give up on anything he started.

Potter too would be after their blood; he had loved his wife and the fat man had found courage from somewhere of late.

The three closed up as they eased their mounts down from the breakneck pace they had set.

'God, we were so close to all that money,' growled Farrier.

'Yeah,' snarled Keever. 'Our troubles started when we decided to go after that Mason hairpin, an' the greaser here talked us into that one.'

Sanchos seemed unconcerned. 'I offered to pay you, *señors*, you accepted. Please do not blame me if you could not do the job.'

'Yeah, that's right,' answered Keever.

'So how did you plan to pay us Mex? Where have you got all this money stashed, huh?'

'It is safe *señor*,' replied Sanchos. 'It is tucked safely away in many banks with only a small amount in each so nobody can get at it but me.' Sanchos smiled at the two men. He would collect the money from its hiding place when he was ready. He had no illusions about his two companions; his life was nothing to them. He knew because he was cast in their mould; he would not hesitate to kill either of them if it showed him a profit.

13

The meal was well under way when Luke Malloy asked Jeff about his recent trip along the Bozeman Trail.

'Never bin up that way myself. Understand it's a fair old distance, runs clear through to Montana I'm told. What's the Indian situation like up that way, Jeff?'

'About what you'd expect if you consider that the land belonged to them in the first place,' replied Jeff evenly. 'Reckon there's gonna be big trouble along the Powder River before long though. We heard a rumour as we were goin' through the area that the army is gonna try to put some staging posts along the trail. Don't reckon Red Cloud or Sitting Bull is gonna be very happy about that an' who can blame 'em?'

'No, guess not,' admitted Malloy.

'The way things are going around here the Texas Rangers are gonna be spread pretty thin on the ground too. Trails are opening up all over Texas. There's cattle being driven along the old Shawnee trail up to a place called Baxter Springs and they tell me there's branches to Kansas City an' Sedalia now.'

'Yeah,' Nathan interjected. 'I heard that Charlie Goodnight and Oliver Loving are cutting a new trail from San Antonio, across the Pecos and clear through the Indian Territories; they're losing some cattle but it ain't only the Indians cutting out beeves. Rustlers are making drovers' lives hell on the trail an' Jesse Chisholm ain't havin' it all his own way either, up Cimarron way.'

'Is all this talk leading somewhere special?' asked Sarah shrewdly. 'Or are you two flapping your lips just to make a noise?'

Luke Malloy grinned, shamefaced. 'Yeah you're right Sarah,' he confessed. 'I was kinda hopin' that Jeff here would be interested in joining us, an' I already primed Nathan to back me up.'

'You should be ashamed of your-selves,' Sarah scolded the two. 'Don't listen to them, Jeff. Just stay here with us and protect your investment. Half of everything we have belongs to you. In a few years you could be a very rich man. We've bought a thousand head of longhorns in dribs and drabs; we're getting 'em at four or five dollars a head but they're fetching twenty-five up Wichita way.'

Jeff held up his hands to ward off the tirade. 'Whoa up there, Sarah,' he exclaimed. 'I don't intend settling down yet awhile, and I don't intend getting tied down in any other way until I catch up with Sanchos. I also have to get to Casa Verde to clear my name of this robbery charge.'

'Ain't no need to do that Jeff,' interrupted Malloy sheepishly. 'Nathan already cleared that. I just kept it going hoping it would drive you my way.'

'Sneaky pair of sidewinders, ain't they, Sarah?' replied Jeff as he sat back contentedly. 'Guess that's the best darned meal I've had in many a long while, Sarah ma'am, sure do appreciate it but I'm gonna have to walk some of it down.' He pushed himself away from the table. 'OK if I take a stroll around?'

'This place is yours,' Nathan replied. 'In fact I think I'll take a stroll too.'

Both Nathan and Luke Malloy climbed to their feet and all three headed for the porch.

'Guess who gets to do the dishes,' groused Sarah.

'Let's all go,' replied Jeff. 'We'll all get stuck into 'em when we come back.'

'*You*, I like!' smirked Sarah as she quickly joined the others. 'We've got something of a surprise for you, young man. Ain't that so Nathan?' she continued, as they strolled around the yard.

'Yeah, we think you're gonna like it too,' replied Nathan, as they stopped by a small corral. 'Well, there he is, Jeff, what do you think?' Nathan waved a hand towards the beautiful black stallion trotting regally around the corral fence.

Jeff was stunned. 'But that was Eli's hoss,' he muttered. 'I can't accept that, it would fetch a hundred an' fifty anywhere. I know your brother's dead, but . . . hell, I just can't . . .'

'Oh yes you can, Jeff,' Sarah broke in. 'Eli is dead now, and he gave us hell when he was alive. But we've bin saving his horse just for you should you ever come this way. We both want you to have it.'

Jeff slipped through the fencing and walked slowly towards the black stallion with one hand extended.

He saw the shiver of contracted muscles run from its neck down its forelegs. It stared at the man in front of him, ears cocked, head up ready to bolt at the slightest sign of danger. Few horses on the range would come to an extended hand, most needed to be caught with a riata. It took a hesitant half-step forward as it blew through its nose.

Jeff stopped, hand still extended. He began talking quietly, coaxingly. The horse blew through its nose again and took another step.

Sarah, Nathan and Luke leaned on the corral poles and watched with bated breath.

The horse seemed to realize that the man was coming no closer. It took a further tentative half-step which put its muzzle over the reaching hand.

Still Jeff did not move. Slowly, as if the horse had decided that this was his new master, it lowered its head until its muzzle touched the proffered hand. Using only the one hand Jeff slowly stroked the muzzle, working gently up to the ears. The horse pushed forward, snuffling softly as it accepted the offer of friendship.

There was an audible sigh behind him as the three relaxed their tense pose.

'You sure have a way with hosses, mister,' muttered Malloy. 'And that's one hell of a horse. What are you gonna call him?'

'Don't rightly know,' replied Jeff. 'Never given a name to a hoss before. Pa always used to follow the Indian way — a hoss was a hoss, didn't need a name.'

'Call him Satan, to remind us all of the black-hearted man who used to own him,' urged Sarah. The venom was always in her voice whenever she mentioned Eli Kyle, the half-breed brother of Nathaniel who had haunted their lives for so many years.

'If that's what you'd like me to call him then that's it,' grinned Jeff. 'You know, I just can't get over all the good things that's happened to me in the last few days: meeting old friends, making a new one. D'you realize that Luke tacked the cost of all these new clothes on your tab, Nathan? An' now I've got me a new bronc as well. It feels good to have such friends again.'

Luke could see the sincerity in the young man's eyes. 'Aw, shucks,' he muttered, glaring at the setting sun almost accusingly to cover his own, and the Kyles' embarrassment.

'Reckon it's time we were getting back to town; be full dark by the time we get there an' I wanna do some persuadin' on the way.'

As they made their way back to the house, Sarah pulled Jeff to one side. 'Don't let that man talk you into anything, son,' she muttered sharply. 'I like him a lot but he has a silken tongue and he don't give up easily.'

'Don't worry, Sarah,' he chuckled. 'I ain't that easy to persuade, an' like I said, nothing's gonna get in the way of my search for Sanchos. I'll be lookin' this way again in a few days, so perhaps you'll keep the horse here for me, huh?'

'Anything you like, just keep coming back, OK?'

Jeff unhitched his mount and swung into the saddle. 'Be seein' you,' he called as he reined away, followed closely by Malloy.

Nathan and Sarah stood on their porch and waved until the two riders melted into the twilight.

'Nice folks,' murmured Luke as he kneed his bronc over the ridge.

'The best,' replied Jeff, as he nudged the roan into a canter.

'People like them are in trouble all over the West you know. Carpet-baggers are movin' in snatchin' land an' property from folks who've lost their kin in the war, taking up grants on land that ranchers have bin usin' for years. Takin' over towns even.'

'You kin stop it right there, Luke,' replied Jeff evenly. 'I've already got a job an' until that sneaky Mex has paid his bill there's nothing you can say that's gonna persuade me to turn off the trail.'

Jeff kicked the horse into a lope to avoid further conversation on the subject.

Luke made his disappointment obvious, staying about half a length behind Jeff as they rode towards town until they heard the steady thrum of horses being ridden at the gallop.

With one accord both riders hauled their mounts to a stop in order to pick up the direction, then they wheeled away to the south, heading directly towards the sound, stretching their mounts to a full gallop.

'In an awful hurry,' shouted Jeff. 'Sounds like trouble.'

'Yup,' agreed Luke, as the horsemen quickly took form in the gloom. 'That's Potter out in front, must be pretty bad fer him to be riding that fast.'

There was no further time for speculation as the riders pulled to a blowing, snorting halt around the two men.

'What gives?' shouted Luke above the noise of the horses.

'All hell's broken loose in town,' someone shouted. 'Keever and Farrier tried to hold up the bank, didn't get any dinero but they shot the teller and George Priest. Killed Potter's missus as well, not to mention the barkeep an' a few others on their way out of town.'

'Said you should have let me finish

my business with that Farrier hairpin,' grunted Jeff almost accusingly. 'I made the mistake of letting that damned Mex off the hook once an' he almost punched my ticket.'

'There was a greaser with these two hellions also,' shouted someone else. 'Threatened Potter's wife and another woman with a machete.'

'*Sanchos!*' the word was torn from Jeff's throat. 'It's got to be that sneaky Mex. Which way did they go?'

Roland Potter was slumped in his saddle saying nothing, his body registering total dejection.

'Hold everything,' shouted Malloy. 'There's no sense in running all over creation; they could have turned off anywhere. We need tracks to guide us. Come on now, let's get back to town, there may be people needing us there. We could be destroying tracks right now and we're gonna need 'em to find the cow-sons.'

Gradually the posse calmed down enough to realize the sense of the argument and began to turn their horses back towards the town.

Luke was watching Jeff, who showed no intention of following his advice.

'What's eatin' you?' he growled.

'Nathan and Sarah's back there,' replied Jeff succinctly. 'I reckon they ought to be warned.'

'I'm coming with you, mister; it might be my chance to get even with the bastards.' The voice brooked no argument and Roland Potter nudged his mount up beside Jeff, who was having difficulty in controlling the big roan as it contracted the excitement of the other horses.

'You sure about this?' Jeff queried.

'It's my right,' replied Potter evenly. 'They killed my wife; I ain't about to go home to an empty house and sleep till morning.' He drove home the spurs. His horse squealed at the unusual treatment before jumping into an immediate gallop.

Jeff spun his horse on a dime and fed spurs. 'See yuh,' he shouted to Luke as he sped away into the darkness after Potter.

'I'm just gonna warn the Kyles,' Jeff shouted as he drew level. 'We don't even know if they came this way.'

'So, let's warn 'em,' growled Potter. 'I might get lucky.'

The fat man showed no sign of slowing the breakneck pace. The thunder of the mad gallop seemed to echo through the silent night as Jeff kept pace with him.

The valley was quiet as they dropped down over the ridge but there was no light in the farmstead. Jeff reached over and dragged on the reins of Potter's horse. Potter tried to shake him off.

'Easy,' growled Jeff. 'There's something wrong down there.'

Potter reluctantly reined in. 'What's with you?' he snarled, eager to ride on.

'Place is in darkness,' muttered Jeff. 'Don't seem likely they'd sit around in the dark.'

'Gone to bed maybe?' Potter spoke doubtfully.

'No, shouldn't think so. I think maybe we should pussyfoot around some before we go charging down there, it don't feel right somehow.'

'What happened to the tough guy?' Potter sneered.

'Ain't nothin' clever about gettin' shot; ain't no satisfaction lyin' in your own blood while they ride off into the night, friend.'

Jeff was already slipping from the saddle as he finished speaking, and Roland Potter quickly followed his example.

'Sorry about that,' he grunted. 'Comes of letting my mouth rule my brains, but they killed my Rosamund and by God I loved that woman.'

'Know just how you feel,' replied Jeff.

'How the hell would you know?' Potter's voice was bitter.

'Tell you about it sometime. Just fer now I guess we'd better slip down to the house on foot. You go in that direction and I'll go this way, best keep plenty of space between us just in case, huh?'

Potter nodded, slid his Winchester from the saddle boot and slipped away.

Jeff was surprised how silently Potter moved for such a big man. Maybe he hadn't always been a businessman. He certainly seemed like a tiger tonight. Jeff shrugged off the vagrant thought as he removed his own Winchester and drifted towards the dark farmhouse.

A dark foreboding was nagging him. What if Sarah and Nathan were lying dead down there and the gang were already putting space between them?

The thought made no difference. The caution instilled in him from years spent in the company of Indians stood him in good stead as he moved forward silently.

Jeff paused. The black horse sprang into his mind. If the gang had been here, Farrier would not have left such a horse behind, it would be against the man's nature.

He began to cut towards the small corral when Nathan's Henry rifle made its distinctive flat crack in the night, quickly followed by three fast, lighter shots from Sarah's 30.30, from a different part of the farmhouse.

A tight grin pulled at Jeff's face, they were both aware of their danger; the Kyles were a formidable couple.

On the heels of the shots a flurry of return fire spat at the farmhouse. Jeff had them spotted almost at once and he began moving towards the gun flashes. Roland Potter was somewhere ahead so he had to be sure that the big man didn't get caught in the crossfire.

The problem was suddenly resolved: Potter seemed to go berserk in his grief and anger. A rifle began firing as fast as the loading lever could be operated, but even above the racket Jeff could hear the fat man screaming curses as he fired shot after shot. He was making no attempt to avoid detection as he ploughed through the scrub and bushes towards the hidden men with all the delicacy of a charging buffalo.

After the first startled curse from the hidden men they turned their attention to this new threat. With cool deliberation they pumped shot after shot into the huge body, which seemed to absorb the bullets as a sponge absorbs water. Yet still the man continued to crash through the brush. His rifle was empty now, but the loading lever was still snapping. Open, close, click, open, close, click, until he finally crashed to the ground, just yards from the two killers.

Jeff had moved forward quickly under cover of Roland Potter's desperate last attempt to reap his vengeance. He was now within a few yards of the hidden men.

'Where the hell did he spring from?' asked Keever in a hoarse whisper.

'Search me,' replied Farrier. 'I just hope there ain't no more surprises out there.'

'Just the one, mister!'

The two men stiffened. 'Who the hell

154

was that!' snapped Keever, in shocked tones.

'You even try to lift those rifles an' you'll find out,' snapped Jeff. 'Drop 'em now!'

The rifles clattered to the ground.

Knowing he could not be seen, Jeff placed his own rifle on the ground before slowly standing up so that his own outline could be seen by the two men.

Jeff had not asked them to raise their hands, so with one accord they made their play.

Jeff had already assessed the two men when he had observed them in the forest as part of the posse; he'd seen Keever back down before Farrier's threat, therefore Farrier had to be first.

Jeff's guns lifted from their holsters with eye-defying speed, at the same time he dropped into a crouch, making himself as small a target as possible, while throwing his antagonists into sharp relief against the lighter shades of the sky.

Farrier was fast, very fast but he was just the merest fraction behind Jeff. Two bullets punched their way into his stomach as his guns levelled. The bullets seemed to paralyse Farrier's reflexes as he teetered up on his toes, guns pointing towards the ground.

Keever managed to get off one shot which passed between Jeff's arm and body, tugging at the new vest as it sped on its way.

Jeff's left-hand gun beat a three-bullet tattoo over Keever's heart. The man was dead before he reached the ground.

In spite of the two bullets in his stomach Farrier was still trying to get off a shot but the paralysis still held him in its vice-like grip.

Jeff watched his efforts dispassion-ately, sixgun poised for immediate action. Farrier's knees slowly became unhinged and he fell forward, face down in the dirt.

Jeff stared at the two men, a tic of worry pulling at his jaw as unanswerable questions flashed through his mind.

Where was Sanchos? Was that sneaky Mex going to get away yet again? There had been no sound from the farmhouse since that first flurry of shots, yet he dare not walk openly towards the building. Sanchos might still be out in the brush somewhere, waiting his opportunity to nail him, or worse, had he already entered the farmhouse?

Even while the chaotic thoughts were chasing each other through his brain, Jeff was instinctively moving towards the silent building, the cold rational side of his mind absorbing every sound, every tiny detail, looking for that one different noise, even the smallest whisper of sound that would spell danger.

He paused crouched like a cougar, in the last bunch of scrub. Ahead of him stretched the front yard, almost 200 yards of open ground.

The moon was breaking over horizon lighting up the area. It would be suicide to attempt crossing that open expanse without protection. 'Damn the moon,' Jeff muttered, then paused. The moon gave him an idea; if Sanchos was around there was one thing that would set the old superstitions working, one thing the Mexican always feared.

Jeff lifted his head and started the sobbing mournful howl of the timber wolf, softly at first then gaining in volume until it gradually drifted away on the night, just the way he had been taught as a young man by Eagle Eye, chief of the Oglala Sioux.

On the heels of the sound Jeff heard Sarah's sharp cry from the farmhouse, followed by breaking glass.

Reacting instinctively Jeff made a zig-zagging run across the yard, guns poised for instant action. He heard a flurry of hooves from somewhere at the rear of the building, but he chose to ignore it until he had discovered the reason for Sarah's cry.

The door crashed open under his charging shoulder as he catapulted into it. Rolling across the room he finished up by the far door regaining his feet with the smoothness of a great cat, eyes and guns probing for danger.

By the light of the moon shining through the windows he saw Sarah bending over a still form on the floor, she was looking fearfully over her shoulder at him.

'Sarah! It's me, Jeff!' he called urgently from the shadows. 'Where's Sanchos?'

14

Sanchos Alvarez pushed his skewbald stallion along at a full gallop, dragging the big black stallion behind him on a lead rope as he left the Kyle homestead.

His mind was in a turmoil. The fates were against him at every turn.

'*Madre de Dios*,' he muttered. 'Everywhere I go I meet El Lobo or his friends.'

It had not been his idea to raid the farm for horses and whatever else might be around, but his avaricious nature would not allow him to refuse the possibility of something for nothing.

Once it had been decided, he had circled around the back of the farm allowing his compatriots to make a frontal assault.

He had been delighted to find the black stallion in the small corral. Quickly he had fashioned a hackamore and slipped it over the beast's head ready for his departure. Then he had ghosted up to the rear window opening. The shutters had not yet been closed so he was able to slip inside.

It was then that he heard the sounds of shooting from the front and heard the reply from the house.

Under cover of the noise Sanchos slipped from the kitchen into the passage leading to the large front room. Two people were in there; he heard them muttering to each other.

Sanchos slid his machete from its sheath with one hand, and palmed his Colt with the other. Two people; the fact that one seemed to be a woman made it even easier, he could kill both, silently, with his machete. It would give him time to hunt around for any gold or coin before his compatriots could take everything for themselves.

The Mexican stepped into the room the machete raised, ready to strike. He stopped in mid-stride as the woman said something.

Sanchos recognized the voice!

Then, on the heels of the thought, he heard the long, low, sobbing wolf howl rising and falling, steadily increasing in volume.

'*El Diablo!*' The words were torn out of him. In the same second, by the dim light of the rising moon, he recognized the big man in front of him, just as Sarah screamed.

Sanchos turned to run but the big man was in his way so he lashed out with his machete as he attempted to dodge past.

The flat of the blade slapped against Nathan's face with terrific force and the knife edge sliced into his neck, but Sanchos didn't care. He was past the man and running, diving through the open window. Sanchos was on his feet in seconds. Grabbing his mount's reins he threw himself into the saddle and snatched the trailing hackamore rope, forcing the black stallion into a mad gallop as he raced away, rowelling the skewbald unmercifully.

Sanchos had already changed saddles twice in his breakneck run and now he was cinching on for the third time. He had travelled far and fast in his mad dash towards Stantonville where he had hidden the money he had stolen from the Casa Verde bank hold-up. Then a two-day ride would put him over the Rio Grande and into Mexico where, with the money he had stolen, he would change from an outlaw into a rich *patron*, he would buy land and men. Even such a *malo hombre* as the *gringo*, Mason, would be unable to touch him then.

As Sanchos continued his race for the border he thought how lucky he had been when he had fallen over the cliff two years ago in the Dakotas.

Mason had almost caught him then. The bullet had grazed his face making him step backwards with a shout of pain and he had fallen into space. But his body had touched a ledge only ten feet from the top and he had rolled into a natural slit in the rocks. His arm and hand had been gashed by the fall leaving a trail of blood on the stone.

By sheer good fortune Sanchos had been hidden from sight, but he was amazed that Mason had not looked for him more thoroughly. He had cowered for hours in his sanctuary before venturing out and retrieving the $20,000 he had hidden in the small coulée below.

Too late Sanchos realized that Mason really thought he had been killed in the fall; if he'd only known, Sanchos could have disappeared into Mexico two years ago; instead, he was, once again, running from the only man he had ever feared.

15

'Oh Jeff, thank God,' Sarah cried. 'Nathan's hurt. If it hadn't been for that wolf howl we'd both be dead. It seemed to scare the living daylights outa that darned Mex.'

Realizing the danger was past, Jeff was already at her side quickly examining Nathan by the light of the moon. The man was unconscious but breathing. He shook Sarah's arm. 'Get a light, ma'am, an' let's see what ails him,' Jeff urged.

Sarah was on her feet in an instant, and within moments she returned with a kerosene lamp burning brightly. There was a heavy bruise on the right side of Nathan's face and a long clean cut which was bleeding profusely on the side of his neck but there was no other sign of injury.

Sarah was all action now, ordering

Jeff to carry her husband into the main room while she hurried upstairs and threw down some pillows and blankets. A sheet was quickly torn into strips and in no time Sarah was stripping off Nathan's shirt ready to deal with the cut which was still pumping blood.

'Get me my sewing bag; it's sitting beside the rocker over there. Gonna need a few stitches here or I miss my guess,' she muttered.

Jeff collected the bag. There was a wry grin on his face as he handed it to her.

'Something funny?' she asked, her voice brittle.

'Yeah.' Jeff continued grinning. 'Last time he got grazed I remember he said he was gonna play it to the hilt, looks like he's gonna get his chance now.'

'With this little nick?' snorted Sarah derisively as she threaded a needle with a thin strip of catgut. 'Man, how wrong can a fella get?'

'You God-damned fink!' grunted Nathan shakily. 'Owch!' he grunted as the needle began its work. 'Hell that hurt!'

'Don't blaspheme,' snapped Sarah testily as she started on him in earnest. 'Big galoot like you won't hardly miss a morning's work with this little scratch.'

Neither man was under any illusions about Sarah's true feelings however, and Nathan felt the warmth of a tear or two fall on his bared chest as Sarah completed the repair and bandaged it. 'That little scratch cost us a good bed-sheet,' she muttered as she finished the bandaging. 'Darned oil lamp is playing the devil with my eyes too,' she grumbled, as she wiped them with a piece of the bed-sheet.

'How's about a cup of arbuckle?' Jeff asked, as he helped her to her feet.

'Would just about hit the spot, son,' answered Sarah. 'Reckon the Mexican's long gone; that timber wolf scared the hell outa him. He'd crept up on us with that damned machete in one hand and a gun in the other; I reckon we were shaking hands with Saint Peter when that wolf sounded off. The Mex seemed to shrink, then he made a dash for the door an' that big lug had to try stopping him . . . '

'How long does it take to make a cup of Java?' Nathan interrupted. 'Man could plumb die of thirst waitin', an' me at death's door.'

There was a plaintive wail from the bedroom. 'See,' muttered Sarah as she hurried towards the stairway. 'Just like his father, sleep through a thunderstorm, but if he's hungry young Jeff will let the world know about it.'

16

The sun was just lifting over the horizon when Sheriff Malloy rode into the yard. Jeff was already standing just inside the front door waiting for him to dismount.

'No posse?' Jeff asked.

'Didn't figger I'd need one, the three of us should be more than enough.'

'You're a bit late Luke, guess most of the chore is already taken care of,' replied Jeff, as they both entered the main room.

'The hell you say?' replied Luke, startled.

'Don't blaspheme,' snapped Sarah. 'Take your hat off and sit! Breakfast is about ready.'

'Could smell it as I came over the ridge yonder,' grinned Luke appreciatively, as he complied. 'What's this about me bein' too late?'

'Keever, Farrier an' the Mex, San-chos, attacked us last night,' answered Nathan as he walked into the room. 'Gave me this,' he grumbled, as he indicated the bandage around his neck. 'Not that I received any sympathy from anybody of course.'

He slid into the third chair while Sarah bustled around dishing up eggs and bacon with liberal helpings of beans and pancakes.

Sarah snorted her derision. 'Sympathy! He was crying worse than a yearling with nappy rash,' she laughed, as she placed a jug of molasses on the table and sat down to eat.

'Anyway, Jeff stopped Keever an' Farrier, they're out there in the brush somewhere,' continued Nathan, ignoring Sarah's interruption.

'Dead?' asked Luke.

'As they'll ever be. The Mex got away, but not before he left me this.' Nathan pointed to his neck again.

'Bad is it?'

Sarah snorted again. 'Six stitches was

all it took, but to hear him talk he almost lost an arm. Worst part was that the Mexican took Jeff's new hoss before he rode off like the Devil himself was snapping at his heels.'

'See what I mean?' complained Nathan forlornly. A horse gone, that's tragic; me wounded, nothing!'

Luke interrupted the general laughter the comment evoked. 'What happened to Mister Potter?'

'He just went mad out there, charged at Farrier and Keever, paid the price in spades,' replied Jeff.

Sarah and Nathan stared at Jeff. 'You mean he's dead out there?' asked Sarah in disbelief.

''Fraid so,' replied Jeff quietly. 'Didn't tell you-all at the time, figgered you had enough to deal with, an' anyway there's nothin' anyone can do about it, dead is dead. I found that out a long time ago.'

'That's true,' agreed Malloy. 'Still, he should be taken into town for a decent burial alongside his wife.'

'We'll take care of that,' muttered Nathan. The mood was downcast after Jeff had told them his startling news and the meal continued in a strained silence.

'You ridin' with me after this Mex, Jeff?' asked Luke, more to break the melancholy silence than the need to enquire.

'I'll take care of it my way,' answered Jeff evenly. 'None of this would have happened if you'd let me take care of my own business two days ago.'

'Sorry you feel like that, son, but breakin' the law is just that. The law don't take sides.' He reached forward and placed a badge in front of the angry young man. 'If you go after the Mex do it with a badge,' he urged. 'You don't have to wear it, in fact it would be better out of sight, but carry it, huh?'

Jeff fiddled with it for a while undecided.

'There's plenty of people needin' help out there,' Luke Malloy urged, seeing Jeff's hesitation. 'You could help stop some of the killing, and be paid for it to boot. Remember, there's still a Wanted flyer out on you. Although it's bin withdrawn it'll take quite a time before all the little towns and villages up and down the country know the true story, an' there's always the bounty hunters.'

Jeff picked it up and tucked it into his vest pocket. 'OK, I'll carry it, but if it gets in the way of me finding that sneaky Mex I'll damn well throw it away. You understand that Luke?'

For once Sarah did not chastise Jeff for his blasphemy. As she stared from one face to the next she could see how deeply serious they all were.

Roland Potter's death hung like a cloud over the conversation. There was no light banter at the table now.

Jeff could judge from Sarah's expression that she was silently praying that Nathan would be staying with her and their young son. He was well aware of the years the two had roamed the country, afraid of what tomorrow might bring. Her one constant wish had been to settle at last in their new home and bring up their child together.

As soon as he reasonably could, Jeff pushed back his chair and climbed to his feet. 'Thanks Sarah,' he murmured. 'That sure was great. Sorry I have to go but you know how it is.'

'I know, son,' she interrupted quietly. 'I guess it's got to be done.'

'You know it has Sarah,' Nathan answered her. 'You want I should come along Jeff?'

Jeff felt Sarah's eyes on him, silently pleading. 'Reckon I can take care of one scared Mex on my own Nathan, thanks for the offer though.'

'Ain't on his own,' grunted Luke. 'I have to see an end to this thing, it's the law,' he ended quickly as Mason made to object. 'Come on, son, let's mosey along now. You'll take care of Mister Potter, Nathan?'

'Count it done, Luke,' answered Nathan, as they all made their way into the yard.

'Have a care now,' Sarah admonished them as the two men mounted, swinging their horses away from the hitching rail. 'We'll take care of the cadavers. I don't think Nathan's terrible injuries will stop him digging a grave or two,' she finished, vainly trying to bring a lighter note into the parting.

'You-all take care now,' Nathan called as he slid his arm around Sarah's shoulders. The two men touched their hats in acknowledgement and used their spurs to send their mounts towards the far ridge.

They turned and waved as they topped the rise. Sarah and Nathan waved in return as the two men disappeared over the hill.

'You got any idea at all where we're headin'?' asked Luke.

'Yup,' replied his companion. 'Met up with a feller named Riley, told me he had to meet a Mex in a place called Stantonville.'

'What happened to this Riley feller?'

'Oh, he died.'

'People seem to die right sudden around you.'

'You think so?'

'Sure do.'

'You comin'?'

'Where?'

'Stantonville.'

'I'm comin',' replied Luke succinctly as he fed steel to his mount and galloped along beside his friend.

'You ever bin to Stantonville?' Luke shouted above the thrum of hooves.

'Nope.'

'Ain't a town at all, just a few worn-out shacks an' Mex cantinas close to the border. The *mimbreños* raid it every so often, just for the fun of it I reckon, mostly to take any womenfolk they happen to find . . .'

'So?' interrupted Jeff.

'Right talkative cuss, ain't yuh? Bet you're a right gabby son once you really get goin'.'

'On the other hand I bet most folk call you silent Luke Malloy, huh?' grinned Jeff.

'I was just explaining . . . '

'So I heard. If we have to cross the Rio to find Sanchos best keep your mouth closed or you'll take on a lot of water.'

'How the blue blazes did I ever get stuck with you?' grumbled Luke.

'*You* didn't, you insisted on comin' so *I'm* the one who's stuck with *you*! Though what I did to deserve such punishment I don't know.'

'I have to tell you we ain't gonna be very welcome in Stantonville,' continued Luke, deliberately ignoring the jibes. 'There's no law an' the population is nearly all men on the run, so we could be getting shot at both comin' and goin'.'

'So?'

'There you go again, runnin' off at the mouth,' grumbled Luke. 'I just wondered if you-all had any special plans once we get there.'

'Yep.'

'Do tell.'

'Find Sanchos and bury him afterwards, if we get the time. Collect my black hoss and ride off into the sunset, that suit yuh?'

'That's a *plan*!'

'It's mine; what's wrong with it?'

'Not very complicated is it!'

'Keep it simple, that's my motto.' Jeff eased his horse down to a canter as they entered the forest.

'Can't think of anything simpler, just hope it works,' grunted Luke. 'Pity you didn't include bringing some vittles while you were working on your plan, eating always makes me feel better.'

'Talkin' does, that's fer sure,' grunted Jeff. 'We'll catch somethin' to eat when we're ready.'

'I know that,' grumbled Luke. 'But it would have been easier if we'd brought some grub with us, huntin' takes time.'

Jeff's hand flipped down and up. On the heels of the shot a cottontail took its last leap into the air. 'Supper,' grunted

Jeff. 'Didn't take long did it!' He slid quickly from the saddle, collected the rabbit and was mounted again while Luke was still wondering what the hell had happened.

Jeff passed the rabbit to Luke. 'I caught it, you cook it.'

'You're hell on wheels with that gun,' murmured Luke. 'Almost as good as me.'

'You reckon?' replied Jeff as he pushed his mount into a fast canter.

'Maybe even faster,' answered Luke.

'Just as well we don't have to try then. Hope you ain't got any fancy ideas about taking Sanchos to jail.'

'Why?'

'You'll be out of luck.' There was the faintest hint of a threat in Jeff's voice. 'I've looked for that sneaky Mex for a long time, so don't get in my way when I find him.'

'You're wearing a badge now.'

'So take it back. That Mex is mine, you understand that, Luke?'

'We'll see. First we have to find him,

what happens after, who knows?'

'I know.'

Jeff eased his mount ahead of Luke, thereby effectively cutting off any further conversation.

17

Sanchos Alvarez eased slowly into the mean-looking, lawless town of Stantonville.

No one was safe here. The last badge-toter who had ridden into town, stayed, permanent! There was a mound in the rise on the outskirts of the town to prove it.

The Mexican stared down the dirt road as he entered. In the dim light of the fast closing evening he could see where the clapboard shacks stopped. That was it — the other end of town! Beyond those shacks was scrub grass and mesquite clear to the border.

Sanchos breathed a quiet sigh of relief as he turned into one of the side streets heading for the disreputable cantina where he had lodged a few days ago.

Any Mexican who was unfortunate

enough to encounter a gang of whites on main street could expect to be robbed and probably beaten. Sanchos had no doubt that he would lose the two superb horses should he encounter any of the white thieves, and he had much more to lose than that. So, it was with great relief that he reined in at the cantina and dismounted.

The *patron* knew he would pay well, and his horses would be kept in the private stables of the cantina until he was ready to make the last run for the Rio Grande. From there to Piedras Grande — the border village would be just the place to collect the kind of men he needed — then ride for Chihuahua.

Once there he, Sanchos Alvarez, would come into his own.

All he needed to do now was to recover his money from its hiding place and cross the Rio Grande before the troublesome *mimbreño* Apache raided this miserable huddle of buildings again. The *federales* might be a problem, but he was sure that he could elude them at the border. From Piedras Grande onward there would be no likelihood of him being stopped by the *federales*.

Sanchos led his horses into the privacy of the stables. The young Mexican hostler bowed, no doubt remembering the lavish tips he had received from the *vaquero* on his last visit. '*Buenos tardes, señor*,' he murmured. 'Again I have the honour of attending your most excellent *caballo*.'

Sanchos smiled. 'See, I have another beautiful *caballo* for you to tend *muchacho*. What do you think of him, eh?'

'Oh *si señor*,' replied the lad, as he eyed the black stallion with admiration. 'It is indeed a beautiful animal, be assured I will give it my best attention.' The young Mexican took the reins and started to lead it into a stall.

Sanchos frowned. '*Momento por favor*. This is not the stall I used the last time I was here, I would like the same stall just as I told you before I left.'

'But, *señor* there is no difference between them,' protested the lad. 'I . . .'

'Enough!' snapped Sanchos. 'How much did I pay you to keep that stall for me?'

'You were indeed very generous, *señor*,' replied the young hostler, dipping his head in respect. 'A whole silver dollar no less. But . . .'

'How much do you earn in a week in this hole?' interrupted Sanchos.

'Not even one dollar, *señor*,' muttered the unfortunate lad.

'Then either give me my silver dollar or do as I ask,' snapped Sanchos, his eyes flashing with anger.

'*Si, si,*' muttered the lad as he scurried to the stall at the end of the line and led the two horses occupying the stall into the gangway.

The moment the young man had moved the horses Sanchos hurried to the stall and quickly looked around. The hostler, although young, was good at his job, the stables had a good layer of clean straw on the floor.

He waited until the lad entered the stall higher up, leading the horses he had removed from the disputed stall.

The moment he was out of sight, Sanchos hurried to one corner and moved the layer of straw with his foot. The big flagstone in the corner had not been moved since he himself had lifted it in the dead of night on his last visit.

Sanchos quickly kicked the straw back into place and strolled into the gangway in time to see the lad unsaddling his tired skewbald.

'A good rub down and some corn as well as oats, Jose,' Sanchos said pleasantly, as he unstrapped his bedroll and carbine. 'Look after them well *muchacho* and I will give you another silver dollar before I leave.'

'*Si, señor*,' he muttered gratefully, obviously very puzzled by the man's quick change of mood. 'They will receive my very best treatment, *señor*.' Jose bowed respectfully to his benefactor as Sanchos swaggered across the alley and into the cantina where the *patron* hurried forward wiping the sweat from his face with a dirty-looking cloth.

'Greetings, greetings, señor,' he said, with a wide ingratiating smile.

'You kept my room?' asked Sanchos regally.

'*Si*, as you requested, señor.'

'I am very tired, I shall go to my room and I have no wish to be disturbed, *comprende*?'

'*Si, señor*; but would you not like something to eat or drink before you retire?' the *patron* asked hopefully.

'I am very tired, I just wish to sleep.' Sanchos brushed the man aside and slowly climbed the stairs to his room.

The doors were not fitted with locks, such a luxury was unknown, so he carefully wedged a chair under the handle. Dropping his bedroll beside the rickety bed with his carbine placed on the top of the bundle close to his right hand, he lay down on the bed, fully clothed and quickly drifted into a deep sleep.

It was pitch dark when he was roused by a slight scuffling sound as someone tried to open the door.

The carbine was in his hand in an instant as he slipped silently from the bed and ghosted over to the door.

He heard the handle turn and someone pushed, trying to open the door. He heard a voice made almost indistinguishable through the thickness of the door harshly whispering.

'*Señor*, please wake up, I must speak with you.'

'*Quién es usted?*' demanded Sanchos.

'*Señor*, please open the door. It is I, Jose. I cannot speak out here, the *patron* might hear me.'

Sanchos slid the chair away from the door.

'Come in carefully *muchacho*,' he warned. 'If there is anyone else with you, you will die. *Comprende?*'

The door opened slowly and Sanchos could see a very frightened white face even in the darkness.

Once Jose was in the room Sanchos quickly closed the door and replaced the chair.

'Stay there until I light the lamp,' he murmured.

'No *señor*, do not light the lamp,' pleaded Jose. 'It will shine into the alley and the *patron* will be alerted. He will beat me unmercifully if he discovers I have been here.'

'Why are you here?'

'I do not understand, *señor*. I happened to mention that you insisted upon having the same stall for your *caballos* although the stall was already being used and he did a most unusual thing. Instead of beating me he patted my arm and gave me twenty centavos.'

'This is unusual?'

'*Si*, in all the time I have worked here the *patron* has never ever given me so much as one centavo, and now twenty!'

'Where is he now, Jose?'

'He has taken his two brothers out to

the stables. I watched without the *patron* knowing as they removed your *caballos* from the stall, then they swept it clean. This I do not understand, for did I not change all the straw only this morning? I . . . '

'*Si, si* I understand, *muchacho*,' Sanchos interrupted the tirade. 'You have done very well indeed *mi amigo*. I must go now. Wait here; when I return I shall reward you handsomely.'

Sanchos was already edging out of the door as he was speaking.

'But *señor*,' protested the boy. 'Maybe I . . . '

'Just do as I say,' Sanchos snapped, his agitation making his voice sharp. 'I must go, *muy pronto*!'

Sanchos hurried away. He could tell what had happened as if he'd been there.

The *patron* had pricked up his ears when the lad had told him that he, Sanchos, had demanded the same stall. The *patron* knew Sanchos for a very rich man; after all had he not tipped everyone most generously? Too generously it would seem.

His room had been searched the last time he had stayed at the cantina, and so had his bedroll and saddle-bags, but they had found nothing.

Sanchos moved swiftly and soundlessly down the stairs, through the adobe archway and across the valley. He could hear muttered grunts and curses as he entered the stables.

Sanchos heard the crash of a stone slab as someone threw it to one side, and more curses, coupled with a harshly whispered warning from the *patron* to make less noise.

The Mexican ghosted up to the stall. Most of the slabs had been removed already and were stacked or thrown into a pile. The three men working in the flickering light of the kerosene lamp were sweating and cursing as they pulled up yet another slab and tossed it aside.

'Are you sure this is where he keeps his money, Carlos?'

'Where else?' snapped the *patron*. 'Why should he become angry when Jose started to put his *caballos* in the wrong stall? We searched everywhere when he was last here, so this is the only place left.'

'Well, at least there are only three slabs left,' muttered the third man. 'We shall soon know.'

They bent over the next large slab and Sanchos pumped the lever of his carbine.

The three men froze at the ominous sound.

'You are working late, *patron*,' Sanchos said coldly. 'Please stay just the way you are or I shall have to shoot you.'

From their crouched position one man could easily reach the lantern. His hand flicked out, knocking the lamp over, at the same time he dived towards it turning, and reaching for his holstered gun.

Sanchos shot him twice before he had fully turned.

The other two followed their brother's lead, diving in different directions as darkness enveloped the stables, while Sanchos threw himself to the ground and rolled behind the boards separating the stalls.

Gunfire roared in the confines of the stall as the darkness was suddenly relieved by a flicker of light.

The lantern had not been extinguished by the fall: the kerosene had poured out of the broken glass base and a flicker of flame had followed its path to the straw in the next stall.

Flames leapt into the air as the horse in the stall let out a squeal of pure terror and began kicking madly at the boards.

Sanchos saw the two brothers through the smoke and flames as indistinct shadows, each crawling towards the opening where Sanchos lay in wait.

Carlos was the first to break. Screaming curses he dashed forward firing his gun as fast as he could pull the trigger.

He stood no chance. With cool deliberation Sanchos shot him, once in the chest then in the head.

By this time the other horses in the stables had joined the first one in their frantic, screaming desire to get away from the smoke and flames. Side boards were crashing down as hooves beat a tattoo on them.

Then the other brother's nerve broke. With an insane screech of terror he dashed across the stall and dived between the boards, landing in a ball under the already demented horse, with flames licking at his clothes.

The animal went berserk, kicking and slashing at the thing under him with its steel-shod hooves.

The man screamed and screamed again as the animal pummelled him into the ground, turning flesh and bones into a bloody pulp.

Sanchos could hear Jose shouting and coaxing at the same time, as he risked his life to cut the horses free and send them galloping into the alleyway and safety.

Ignoring the searing heat Sanchos hurried to the corner slab. It took all his strength to lift it and throw it aside. Snatching out the two burlap sacks, already smouldering with the heat, he turned to run out of the stall. The bottom of one sack split under the weight and several silver dollars slipped out, glistening enticingly in the flames.

Sanchos looked up as something crashed into the stall door.

Jose was standing there, his clothes smoking, hair almost all singed away. But what Sanchos saw was his eyes, big and round, staring in satisfaction at the glistening pile of silver dollars on the floor.

Sanchos knew there was no way the lad would be able to keep what he knew to himself, and if Jose told anyone he would have all the thieves in Stanton-ville after him before an hour had passed.

As these thoughts slid swiftly through his mind, he croaked, 'Have you managed to get my *caballos* out, *muchacho*?'

The boy nodded, his gaze riveted to the money on the ground. His eyes slowly raised to the two sacks in the Mexican's hand.

Sanchos could read his thoughts like a page in a book: if there were so many coins on the floor, how many could there possibly be in those two large sacks?

The Mexican could not use his rifle, it was in the hand holding the bags, nor could he draw the sixgun for the same reason.

His left hand dipped for his machete; it flickered in the flames like a serpent's breath as it travelled across the stall. The boy did not even realize what was happening. He died instantly as the spinning blade split his skull from crown to neck.

Such was the power of the throw that it continued onwards and buried itself in the boards beyond.

Mere seconds had passed since the

lad had looked into the stall, but the heat was getting more intense by the moment.

Sanchos scraped up as much of the fallen money as he could and stuffed it into his pockets. He closed the opening in the broken bag and rushed for the alley, snatching his machete as he passed, not even sparing a glance at the boy who had taken the trouble to warn him of his employer's perfidy.

Timbers were crashing around him as he burst into the alley. The fact that the outer walls of the stables were built of adobe, as was the cantina and the alley between, was all that saved him from certain death.

It was also fortunate that he was in the Mexican quarter, the whites would not bother to help put out the fire, they were more likely to add timber to the flames.

Sanchos hurried to his two horses, snatched up the first saddle and blanket that came to hand and strapped it on the skewbald.

Ignoring his gear still in his room he grabbed a second blanket and wrapped the two sacks inside it. Strapping it behind his saddle he grabbed the black's lead rope, mounted, and rode swiftly away before anyone could cause him any delay, or start asking the kind of questions he had no wish to answer.

Sanchos glanced over his shoulder as he breasted the rise on the outskirts of town, up there where the unknown lawman had been buried.

There was a deep red glow where the stables had been. He saw sparks spill from the cantina. There would be nothing left but the adobe walls by morning.

He turned his face to the border and kneed the skewbald into a fast trot. 'Two good *caballos* and two sacks of money,' Sanchos muttered. 'I am almost there; a few more days of riding and I will realize my dream.'

18

It was late afternoon the following day when Jeff Mason and Luke Malloy rode towards the main street of Stantonville. It seemed that every man had at least one side-arm strapped to their waists and some carried a rifle also.

'Kinda friendly little town, huh?' grunted Jeff.

'Yeah, looks like a real welcoming committee comin',' replied Luke, nodding to where a businesslike body of men were approaching.

'You get the feelin' they ain't exactly pleased to see us?' asked Jeff.

'Don't look none too happy about it, them guns ain't for decoration.'

'Be a good idea to put some space between us d'you think?' Jeff muttered.

'Yup, let's do that small thing,' replied Luke, edging his mount away from his companion. 'Only don't get lippy, OK?'

The body of men stopped and rifles tilted towards the two riders who obligingly drew their mounts to a halt facing the group.

'Goin' far?' asked a big, bearded man who seemed to be leading the men.

'Who's askin'?' replied Jeff evenly.

The man seemed nonplussed by the answer. He looked over his shoulder as if for support then back again, his confidence returning.

'I'm askin',' he grated as he eased his rifle around so that it pointed more directly at Jeff. 'An' I ain't waitin' long fer your answer, mister.'

'You are about as near to Saint Peter as you're ever likely to get, mister,' Jeff murmured quietly.

'I done told you not to get lippy,' complained Luke through tight lips.

The big man grinned, wiggling the rifle. 'There's an awful lot of us here,' he hinted.

Jeff gave the man a thin-lipped grin

of his own. 'When it's over you won't be around to do any counting.'

The man's grin slipped a little. 'There's just too many of us fer you, son, you'll be dead.'

Jeff's grin widened, showing a confidence he was far from feeling. 'So will you, and at least six others. So if you're feelin' lucky, go to it.'

The big man's smile had vanished now.

'He's bluffin',' growled a man in the second row.

'You reckon?' Luke enjoined. 'Well, I guess I'll mark you down fer one of mine, mister.'

The man suddenly realized that he had placed himself first on the list and began to try to sidle away.

'Don't pussyfoot around, mister,' growled Luke. 'I might decide to start the ball rolling if you make me nervous. His six an' my six means twelve cadavers for boot hill just fer starters. Now suppose you-all calm down an' tell us what the beef is.'

'Somebody tried to burn down the town last night, set fire to a Mex cantina just off main street. We figured you might have come back fer a second try,' someone shouted.

The excuse was weak, but at least it gave the gang a reason for easing off without losing face. They hadn't expected such determined opposition from two cow waddies.

But close up they looked rather harder to chew than they'd first thought.

'Guess you'd best ride on out of town while you're still in one piece,' growled the big man, trying to salvage something of his dented pride. 'Keep ridin' thataway, it ain't far,' he finished, jerking his thumb over his shoulder.

'Ain't in any hurry, feller.' Jeff still had that thin-lipped smile pasted on his face. 'Gonna get me a wash an' some grub. Might even mosey around for a spell 'fore I leave. Should you feel lonesome, mister, look me up. Be a pleasure to do business with you.'

The thin smile had not left his face and his voice was still quiet and even as he stared at the big man but there was menace in every word. 'Now spit or close the window, mister, I'm through talkin' an' so are you.'

Jeff gigged the big roan forward and the gang eased slowly apart to allow the two men through.

'I *told* yuh not to git gabby,' complained Luke. 'D'you realize how many guns that bunch of shits had?'

'Yeah, too many. Let's find somewhere to eat, an' I hope you git indigestion. Give you somethin' to really complain about.'

'Did you have to go an' push it all the way? We could have ridden straight on through, no problem.'

'I had a problem.'

'Yeah, what?'

'I'm hungry. I also want to look at that cantina.'

'That was just an excuse to get 'em out of a bind.'

'You didn't smell the smoke?'

'Well, yeah, but that could be anything.'

'Sweet smoke, like cookin' meat,' grunted Jeff. 'Somebody or somethin' was cooked in that fire. It's in the Mexican quarter so I wanna look, OK?'

'Like human meat?'

'Sure was, let's take a look.'

They turned their slow-moving horses into the side road which was really just a wide track. They had no trouble finding the cantina; wisps of smoke were still curling out of the place and it was too hot to enter.

Jeff and Luke dismounted and made their way slowly into the alley between the stables. Even here the heat was catching their breath and the taste of sulphur was strong in the air, as was the sweet, sickly smell of human meat.

Jeff didn't hesitate, kicking glowing hulks of wood aside he walked down the aisle between the adobe wall and what had been the stables, looking carefully into each one in turn.

Luke followed, coughing as the

sulphur entered his nose and throat. 'Don't reckon we'll find anything here,' he muttered from behind a protective bandanna.

Jeff did not reply, merely continued to stare into each stall in turn. He stopped at the last one and stared speculatively at the pile of flagstones, trying to understand why they were all stacked on one pile. The smell was stronger here.

He glanced around a second time. The pile of ash beside where the door used to be smelled even more strongly. He picked up a still smouldering piece of timber and pushed at the pile. A small skull rolled out.

Jeff heard a sharp intake of breath as Luke saw it. 'Small skull, boy or a young man got roasted here.'

'Skull is split almost in two,' added Jeff succinctly. '*Machete!*' The word seemed to be snatched from him. It linked him with Sanchos and although he was well aware that most Mexicans liked the machete, in his mind it had to be Sanchos.

He moved farther into the stall and found two more piles of ash. He poked them experimentally, once again bones showed beneath the ashes covering the mounds.

Slowly Jeff walked to the far corner, piecing together what must have happened here. He saw the excavation in the corner and called Luke over.

'Reckon Sanchos hid the money under this slab, somebody found out and came to find it. Sanchos caught 'em.'

'You don't know that,' protested Malloy. 'How about the boy?'

'Reckon he came in while Sanchos was killin' the men who wanted his loot so the Mex split his skull. The boy was just unlucky.'

'Unlucky is puttin' it kinda mild,' replied Luke.

Jeff had moved away from the corner, giving every square inch of the floor his careful scrutiny.

Suddenly he stopped and crouched,

blowing away the covering of ash on the floor. He attempted to pick something up but dropped it with a curse as it singed his fingers.

'What is it?' asked Luke.

'One very hot silver dollar,' replied Jeff as he moved the ash around with his piece of timber. 'Sanchos had the loot that was stolen from Casa Verde here; some of it was in silver dollars and the rest was paper money. Reckon he dropped some and the kid saw it on the floor, so he had to die.'

They were both sweating profusely by this time and the breath was rasping harshly in their throats.

'What say we get outa this hell-hole an' breathe some decent air fer a change,' grumbled Luke. 'I could sure sink a pint of something cool right now.'

Jeff nodded curtly. He ignored the three silver dollars on the floor. Some kid would come in here searching when the place had cooled off and leave thinking he was a millionaire.

Sanchos was still out there somewhere, and Jeff intended to find him if he had to follow the trail to the back end of Hell.

Both men sucked in lungfuls of clean air as they walked towards their mounts. Luke wiped sweat from his face and neck with his bandanna. Jeff didn't untie the dark red neckerchief around his own neck. He never removed it except when he was alone. The scars under it were his own private burden; the marks would be there for the rest of his life and he had no wish to be gawped at because of them.

They walked slowly down the main street leading their mounts. The stink of sulphur was beginning to leave their throats at last.

Jeff sniffed appreciatively. 'That smell like steak to you?'

'Nothin' but,' replied Luke. 'Sure makin' the old taste buds work overtime. What say we go an' hog-tie one each?'

'My sentiments exactly,' grinned Jeff

as they came to the source of the mouthwatering smells and tied their mounts to the hitch rail.

They stared into the window. The steak house seemed to be doing a roaring trade, the benches set along trestle tables were filling up fast.

'We lookin' or eatin'?' grunted Luke. 'My stomach's stuck to my wishbone.'

'Eatin'!' replied Jeff. 'Let's get to it, pardner.'

As they entered Jeff saw two men look up then leave in a hurry, their steaks left untouched. 'Don't say much for the cooking here,' he muttered.

'Ain't the cookin',' replied Luke. 'They've recognized me as a lawman, kinda lost their appetite I reckon.'

'Got somethin' to hide, huh?'

'Who ain't in this hell-hole? Would you come here from choice?'

'Reckon not,' replied Jeff. 'But seein' they ain't hungry guess we might just as well help 'em out,' he grinned, as he stepped over the bench and sat in front of an extremely large platter overflowing with a nice juicy steak.

Luke quickly followed his lead. 'You sometimes get some really good ideas,' he grunted. Picking up the knife and fork he cut off a large succulent slice and started chewing appreciatively. 'Sure saves waitin'; there's quite a crowd at the counter.'

'Cheaper too,' grunted Jeff around a mouthful of meat, as he also tucked in with gusto.

It was over an hour later when the two men left the eating house; they had really packed away the food. 'That apple pie was almost as good as Sarah Kyle's,' commented Luke, as he patted his full stomach.

'Yeah,' agreed Jeff. 'That steak was good too.'

'Best kind; ain't often I get a free meal,' grinned Luke as he reached for his tobacco pack and began to roll a quirley. 'What you plannin' to do now?'

'First I'm gonna buy me some vittles, a fry-pan, a bedroll, and stock up on some shells for the guns. Then I'm makin' tracks for the Rio because that's where Sanchos is headed, an' where he goes I'll be right behind.'

'Kinda determined cuss, ain't yuh? Is this Mex worth all the bother? There's a lot of people in Texas you could be helpin' now that you're carryin' a badge.'

'First things first,' grunted Jeff.

'How about we get a room and a good sleep first?'

'In this town? I'd rather sleep under the stars. Could catch something' real nasty in one of those beds, and I don't just mean fleas. You please yourself, Luke, but I'm ridin' on.'

'Real nice of you tuh give me a choice,' grunted his friend. 'Say, I thought you were flat broke?'

'I was, but Nathan insisted that I have some of the money he put by for me. Nice family, the Kyles.'

They unhitched their mounts and led them to the livery. 'Grain 'em and give 'em a real good currying,' Luke instructed the Mexican hostler. 'How much?'

'For the best treatment, *señors*, six bits each.'

'Wasn't planning on leavin' 'em fer a week,' grunted Luke.

The Mexican smiled ingratiatingly as Jeff inspected the stalls. 'As you see, *señor*, my stables are very good, no?'

Jeff nodded. 'I want mine ready to ride at sundown. If you treat my hoss right it's worth a half-dollar American, OK?'

'*Si señor!*' beamed the hostler, looking expectantly at Luke.

'Take no notice of him,' Luke grunted. 'Suddenly he thinks he's a millionaire, comes of never having two cents to his name.'

The Mexican's smile slipped a little, so Luke grinned at him. 'Just funnin' friend. OK, same goes fer me, but make it good, mind.'

'*Si señor*,' shouted the Mexican to the retreating men. 'Your *caballos* will be treated to the very best. *Adios amigos.*'

19

It was full dark by the time the two men had saddled up and strapped their bedrolls and food to their saddles; both had spent some time cleaning and checking their pistols and Winchesters.

The hostler was staying real close as they led their mounts out of the livery, his face showing deep concern in the light of the hurricane lamp he was holding.

The Mexican almost dropped it when the gleam of silver flickered in the lamplight as Jeff flipped the silver dollar towards him.

'*Muchas gracias, señor,*' he said, smiling gratefully as he put the coin between his teeth. Then, evidently satisfied, he slipped the coin into his pocket and swept off his sombrero. '*Vaya con Dios, señors,*' he murmured respectfully.

The two men flipped a salute as they mounted and rode into the darkness.

'A whole dollar,' moaned Luke. 'We could have slept in one of the hotels for a week on less.'

'Hotel my eye, flea pit more like. Anyway, nobody said you had to come, you just offered.'

'Only to keep you out of trouble; them *mimbreños* are raiding all along the border, seems they got a big hate on since they broke out of the reservation.'

'Who can blame 'em, after all it was their land?'

'You an Indian lover, Jeff?' questioned Luke. 'Bet you think all Indians are saints, huh?'

'Nope; Indians are human-beings same as white folk, or black folk too for that matter, there's good and there's bad. Mind you, I've yet to see an Indian as mean as a feller I know name of Luke Malloy . . . '

'Why you miserable sonofabitch, I kitted you out when you had holes everywhere, and paid for a bath when you were nothin' but a walkin' flea pit don't forget.'

'No you didn't, Nathan did.'

'Well I *almost* did,' grumbled Luke.

'Thank God you didn't; I'd have to put up with you havin' nightmares as well as grumbling all the time.'

The steady banter continued until they reached a grove of cottonwoods and mesquite.

'This suit us d'you reckon?' asked Luke.

'Guess so, you set the fire I'll see to the broncs. Figger a nice mug of arbuckle should hit the spot before we settle down.'

The two men went quietly about their chores, and finally, having unrolled their soogans settled down to wait for the coffee to boil.

'Figger to move away from the fire afore I settle down,' muttered Jeff. 'Indians might decide to take a look at the camp.'

'Did you think I was gonna sleep right here?'

'Here we go again,' grumbled Jeff as he leaned forward and poured the hot black arbuckle into the two waiting mugs. 'Where you figger on movin'?'

'Why?'

'Waal if you talk as much in yore sleep as you do other times I don't wanna be too close when the Indians find you,' chuckled Jeff, as he leaned back into his soogans blowing on the hot coffee.

'We gonna put the fire out?'

'Waste of time; they'll smell it if they're around, and by leavin' it burning it'll give 'em something to focus on besides us,' replied Jeff.

'Now who's the gabby one?' answered Luke slyly, as he carried his bedroll into the trees close to his mount.

Jeff tossed the dregs of his coffee mug into the fire, kicked some earth on to the glowing coals and collected his own gear. Then, leading his mount off a short distance, he too set out his bedroll and crawled into the warmth.

There were two almost simultaneous snicks as both men prepared their rifles, then lay back ready for a sleep soothed by the noises of insects and animals of the night . . .

Jeff Mason slowly opened his eyes. He lay perfectly still, it was pitch dark.

Something had disturbed his sleep. His horse had not moved or snorted he was sure because his mind was attuned to such sounds.

The night was still and silent. Too silent, there were no night noises at all! The total lack of sound was in itself menacing.

Moving his head as little as possible he allowed his eyes to scan every possible inch of the area in the immediate vicinity. He could see the darker bulk of Luke's mount which seemed a little restless. Slowly another dark bulk raised itself beside the horse. Jeff's hand slipped to the back of his neck where that paper-thin knife nestled.

Before he could make the throw

there was a slight grunt and the dark form seemed to slump and then sink slowly to the ground.

A second shadow moved swiftly towards Jeff, and he realized that Luke was coming to warn him of the danger, but in doing so he was risking his own life.

Acting intinctively Jeff raised himself high enough to be seen for a brief moment, and Luke faded into the bushes.

There was a rush of displaced air behind him. Jeff rolled swiftly away as a body with the distinctive rank smell of stale animal fat landed beside him. The paper-thin knife slid forward into the Indian's throat and slashed wickedly sideways. A slight strangled cough, and the Indian was dead.

Dimly Jeff could hear Luke carrying out his own wordless fight for life as he snatched up his Winchester and met the second charging Indian with its stock. He felt the warmth of blood spurt in his face as the diving Indian met the swinging rifle; the attacker gave a submissive grunt and collapsed. The butt descended a second time, connecting with the back of the Indian's neck, snapping it like a rotten twig.

Through it all the big roan had stood perfectly still. An Indian tried to use its bulk as cover. The hooves slashed backwards turning the man's head into instant pulp.

So far there had been no gunshots or arrows; doubtless the rest of the band were afraid to fire in case they killed one of their own, but now Jeff could hear arrows snicking and thrumming through the trees.

He rolled behind the bole of a large tree searching desperately for some sign of the attackers. He glanced over his shoulder to where Luke should be and saw a dark shadow raising what appeared to be a tomahawk. Jeff's Winchester spoke twice in .instant reaction.

The moment he had fired Jeff part

rolled and part ran towards the spot where he knew Luke to be. He could hear the flit of arrows clipping leaves and branches around him, his shots had given the attackers a lead on his location.

Jeff dived head first into the shallow depression, eyes searching frantically for any sign of hostiles. There were none; the attack had stopped as quickly as it had started. Jeff lay flat in the depression, keeping perfectly still, depending upon his ears to warn him of danger. The silence was profound.

Jeff dragged himself slowly across the sparse grass in the hollow, the smell of Indian easy to locate.

He passed two and a quick check told him that they would give no further trouble. He crawled over to Luke and allowed his hands to run gently over the still body. His hand lifted gently to Luke's scalp and his questing fingers located a lump as big as a hen's egg. Luke moaned at the touch.

'D'you think you could stop playing with that thing?' he groaned.

Jeff grinned his relief in the darkness. 'Plumb glad they hit you in the one place they couldn't do any damage,' he muttered. 'You OK, apart from that tiny little bump?'

'Tiny, huh?' grunted Luke. 'Feels like I got all the drums in the Union Army banging away inside my skull.'

'It's big enough to take 'em,' came the terse reply.

'You reckon they're gone?'

'Movin' off, probably found us a little too hard to chew. Makin' fer the town now I guess.'

Jeff slowly and cautiously stood up, allowing his eyes to probe as far as possible into the darkness. He picked up a small branch and threw it into the trees; there was no reaction so Luke climbed slowly to his feet.

'Coffee?' asked Luke.

'Might be an idea,' agreed Jeff. 'I'll go fetch the roan. Good hoss that, took one of 'em out real sweet, waited quiet as you like then hit him with both hooves.'

'Thought you liked Indians?'

'Never was much on night visitors red or white,' grunted Jeff, as he walked towards his mount. 'Kick that fire awake; I'll get the arbuckle.'

The balance of the night was spent drinking coffee, and well before dawn they'd eaten a hearty breakfast. Then they settled down to wait for the return of the raiders. Both men knew the Indians would not pass them by when they returned from their raid on Stantonville.

Dawn was making its red blush on the horizon when the two men heard the thrum of ponies' hooves heading in their direction.

They had placed the horses in comparative safety and had made breastworks from fallen branches, carrying the heavy timbers to the very edge of the trees so that the Indians would be robbed of immediate cover. Two good men with the 1866 fast repeating

Winchesters could cause untold damage before the Indians could circle around to find protection.

Luke nodded to Jeff. Neither man needed to speak as they crouched there waiting until the Indians decided to make their charge.

The Apache were superb horsemen and they loved to show off by riding swiftly backwards and forwards just out of range, hoping to coax the waiting men into wasting cartridges.

They soon realized they were wasting their time. Suddenly, as if by common consent, the cavorting ponies turned towards the breastworks. Yipping and howling, the Indians made their charge, firing their carbines ineffectually from the backs of their speeding mounts as they came.

Both men waited, outwardly unruffled by the sight of twenty or so screaming Indians charging towards them, for although the Apache were superb horsemen and excellent with a bow and arrow, they had never learned the art of using a carbine or rifle, especially from the back of a galloping horse.

The two Winchesters spoke almost in unison: six shots and six Indians crashed from their ponies.

Yipping madly the *mimbreño* Apache split both ways running parallel to the breastworks firing one-handed.

Two Indians were using bows, and the arrows were cutting the air close to the two men before they too were shot from their ponies.

Suddenly the riders wheeled away, snatching at loose mounts as they rode past them.

'Reckon that'll do 'em,' Luke said calmly.

'Yep,' replied Jeff as he climbed out of the protection. 'I'm headin' fer Mexico; you coming?'

'Guess so.'

Both men climbed aboard their mounts and rode leisurely through the settling dust kicked up by the Indian ponies. Neither man so much as glanced toward the dead Indians.

20

The wily Mexican could feel the elation rising in him as he crossed the Rio Grande. Eagle Pass was behind him and every time he glanced at the two burlap sacks tied to the saddle of the black stallion he could feel the flutter of fulfilment. A short ride using the two mounts alternately and he would be in Piedras Grande where he would recruit the kind of men he required.

There was no sign of the *federales* as he spurred his mount towards his goal. He would spend a few days there making sure he selected the right men before setting off for Chihuahua.

Life had turned full circle, and now Sanchos Alvarez was returning to the place of his birth with more money than his poor family had ever dreamed of. Sanchos felt good. No more would he have to worry about El Lobo Diablo.

This was his country at last, no longer would he be an outcast.

★ ★ ★

Just two days behind Sanchos Jeff Mason and Luke Malloy rode slowly down through Eagle Pass.

'What makes you so God-damned sure the Mex is still ahead of us?' growled Luke, for the hundredth time. 'He might have seen those Indians and doubled back to Stantonville.'

Jeff just shrugged. 'So I'll have to go back, but I don't think so. Look, nobody's asking you to come along.' Suddenly he raised a cautioning hand. They were close to the crossing and Jeff quickly turned his mount into the concealment of some large boulders.

'What are we stopping for?' grumbled Luke, as he pulled his own mount into the rocks. 'There's nobody around.'

Jeff had his head to one side listening intently, once again he held up his hand asking for silence. Another three minutes passed and Luke was about to speak again. Sensing what he was going to do Jeff held up the hand again and Luke kept his peace.

Then Luke heard it also, the steady thrum of hooves as a troop of *federales* rode by on the opposite side of the river.

'You tellin' me you heard 'em comin'?' Luke asked disbelievingly.

'You think it was luck!' grunted Jeff, as he eased his mount into the river.

'Where we headin' for now?'

'Nearest border town. We'll ask around, if that sneaky Mex hasn't shown himself I'll just ride back into Texas and start lookin' all over again.'

'Don't mind me,' complained Luke, 'I'm just along fer the ride.'

It was high noon as the two men rode into the village. The sun was beating down sucking all the air out of the place. A few men were draped around in rockers with their sombreros over their faces; it was siesta time and nothing was moving anywhere, few even bothered to look up as the two rode slowly down the dusty street to the cantina.

By common consent they both dismounted and entered the comparative cool of the adobe building.

The *patron* looked up lazily. '*Si?*' he asked grudgingly.

'Beers,' grunted Luke tiredly.

'Beers?' questioned the *patron* almost sneeringly.

'You deaf?' asked Luke.

'No *señor*, but *beers?* No tequila?'

'My throat's already burning. I want somethin' to cool it, *comprende?*'

The *patron's* face lit up however when he saw the silver cartwheel on the counter, put there by the other gringo.

'Information, *por favor*,' Jeff said quietly.

The *patron* nodded, his eyes glued to the silver dollar.

'Mexican, last two days, two horses, one a black stallion, you know of him?'

Understanding spread over the man's face. 'Oh *si*,' he grinned hugely. 'You are *pistoleros, si*? But he is only hiring Mexican *vaqueros* who are good with a gun, so he will not employ you, *señors*,' he said apologetically as he swiftly swept the silver dollar into his hand in case they should decide to take it back.

'How many men has he hired?' asked Jeff.

The man shrugged. '*Quien sabe*. This morning he has six, but he has ridden out to the Camille rancho where they are disposing of some men.' He shrugged again. 'He may have all he wants by this time.'

'*Gracias*. Perhaps you could provide us with some food?'

'*Si señor*,' grunted the *patron*. He banged on a wood panel set in the wall and shouted something in fast Spanish that Jeff could not understand and in a few moments a woman scurried out with plates laden with tortillas, meat, chilli beans and peppers.

'Which way do I ride to find the rancho of Camille?' asked Jeff, as he ordered another foaming mug of root beer.

The *patron* obliged with enough directions to find the place fairly easily as there was only the one rancho in the whole valley. 'But, please believe me, *señor*, he is only looking for Mexicans not Americanos,' he finished with an expressive shrug.

'So what now?' asked Luke, as they left the cantina.

'Waal I'm just gonna ride out thataway an' look over the ground, might be just the place to set me a bear trap.'

'You mean we're gonna take on this whole crowd of Mexicans on their own ground, with the *federales* ready to drop on us at any time! D'you realize we ain't even supposed to *be* this side of the border?' protested Luke.

'D'you always moan this way or have you got indigestion from all those beans you ate?'

'No!' replied Luke heatedly. 'I just ain't used to taking on half of Mexico with some mad lobo wolf who just ain't got sense enough to get out of the rain.'

'Ain't rainin'.'

'It will be . . . bullets!'

The dusty, sandy soil they were riding over was hardly capable of raising scrub, and ahead they could see where barren rock climbed to the horizon. The heat-haze reflecting from the sandy soil made the distant hills seem insubstantial.

'Good country to die in,' remarked Luke.

'Yeah, fer Mexicans,' replied his companion laconically. 'Them hills will be just the place to do it too.'

'Admire your confidence,' muttered Luke sarcastically. 'There's probably only about twenty or so comin' back with this Sanchos feller.'

'Yeah, shouldn't be a problem, so long as they don't have a Gatling with 'em,' replied Jeff. 'For a Ranger you're one pessimistic sonofagun, fella. What my mom would call a regular Job's Comforter.'

'You had a *ma*!'

'Sure did.'

'You *do* surprise me; now I can believe anything'.'

The hills were getting closer now, and from a gap to the west of them Jeff spotted a dust cloud.

'Seein' as how you're in a believing mood, Luke, I reckon you'd best look thataway. Unless I miss my guess, that's our Mexican friend and a few of his *vaqueros*. We'd best make tracks for the hills, feller.'

Jeff fed spurs to his mount, and Luke was close behind.

'Thought things were too quiet to last,' Luke yelled as he drew level. 'They've spotted us; they're trying to cut us off.'

Both men leaned low over their mounts' necks in an effort to obtain more speed. Sanchos and his *vaqueros* were cutting across the front of the foothills and both Jeff and Luke realized that it was going to be close. Out here on the open ground they would not stand a ghost of a chance: they had to get into the rocks.

A smattering of shots crackled out from the closely knit bunch of *vaqueros* but nothing fell even close to the two fleeing men.

Luke began to ease his mount eastward. Jeff realized Luke's intentions and followed his lead.

'Never make it runnin' straight,' panted Luke. 'See that slit in the rocks? That's our best bet.'

Another burst of fire came from the bunch as they realized the fugitives' intentions.

'Keep shootin' boys,' muttered Luke. 'While you're shootin' you ain't makin' the best use of your ponies.'

The two swept into the slit in the rocks a mere eighty feet in front of their pursuers and bullets were already ricocheting off the canyon walls around them.

The narrow trail was Y-shaped ahead. By mutual consent each took a different branch. Jeff clattered along the rocky defile. He guessed that the pursuers would not charge into the narrow opening in case the fugitives were waiting for them, so Jeff knew that he had a little time to get set.

He slid his rifle from the boot and dismounted on the run, slapping the horse into even greater efforts as Jeff slipped and stumbled over the uneven surface. As soon as he could stop he dived into the shelter of the huge boulders at the side of the trail.

Keeping the boulders between himself and his pursuers he started to climb as fast as he could.

He was about eight feet above the ground when the first shot spat rock dust into his face.

Jeff dropped out of sight, removed his stetson and peered cautiously down at the trail. Two men were starting to climb towards him. He snapped two quick shots in their direction making them dive for cover. He took advantage of this respite to move to another pile of rocks where he settled down to outwait his opponents.

After a short pause he could hear the two men resume their climb. Jeff smiled grimly. From what he could hear of their conversation, the two *vaqueros* were assuming he had not moved from his original position. A trickle of small stones and dust began falling from above and it warned him that someone was moving around up there.

He heard the distant crackle of rifles and carbines; it sounded as if Luke was getting his share of the attention.

As Jeff was squinting through the light powdering of dust he saw an ornate riding boot reaching from the rock immediately above him, across to the rock in front of him. The unknown man was attempting to cross the slit in the rocks where Jeff was hiding.

He watched, hardly daring to breathe, as the foot gradually found enough purchase to take the man's weight. His other foot followed until he was standing on the rock looking outwards with his back to the man he sought. Slowly, still unaware that there was any danger, the man lowered himself into a crouch, poised on the top of the rock.

Jeff put the barrel of his rifle against the man's backside and gave it a hefty push.

The Mexican catapulted off the rock with a howl of dismay and fear which ended abruptly as he fell among the boulders several feet below.

Jeff heard the two other men scrambling towards their comrade so he eased himself around the boulder hoping to catch them unawares. A bullet spanged off the rock within inches of his face and he felt the whisper of a second shot as it passed between his face and the rock.

Jeff had only seen two *vaqueros* at the outset but it was clear that he had more than that to contend with. He burrowed further back into his niche as another bullet bounced off the rock and ricocheted into the refuge. He backed out of the niche and slid around another boulder. Jeff could now see the one who had almost marked his card.

The man had become bold; certain that he had the quarry cornered, he was closing steadily on Jeff's position. Each time he moved he fired another bullet at the rock allowing it to ricochet into the niche.

Jeff took his time and, as the man fired again, his finger caressed the trigger. Almost as an echo his own rifle answered. The man seemed to flip around as the bullet tagged him, leaving him sprawled over the rocks.

On the heels of his shot the two men below started firing as fast as they could lever bullets into the firing chamber and he had to move fast to avoid the vicious whine of the bullets as they ricocheted in all directions.

As he rapidly climbed the rocks, twisting this way and that to avoid being seen by the men below, his mind was coldly analysing the situation. In the background he could hear the carbines crackling like Chinese firecrackers over where Luke had taken shelter. Then there was the occasional deeper sound of Luke's Winchester.

Jeff hoped his friend had managed to find the time to take some spare cartridges with him because it seemed that he had the larger share of trouble.

Jeff only carried .45 shells in his gunbelt but he resolved that in future he would always fill his belt with both calibres. His own rifle held a further eleven shells, after that he would have to depend on the lesser range of his pistols.

He continued climbing as rapidly as possible, aiming to join forces with Luke by climbing over the ridge and down the other side, but first he had to get the two men behind him off his back.

A quick glance over his shoulder told him that the men were still doggedly climbing.

He slipped behind a large rock which was precariously balanced upon three smaller ones. It did not look as if it would take too much effort to send it tumbling down the rock-strewn slope.

Two more bullets spanged off the rocks, warning Jeff that he was losing time. He sent two of his own in reply, forcing the men to take cover.

He moved behind the huge rock and gave it a tentative push; nothing happened.

He tried a second time, putting more weight behind it; still it remained stubbornly in place. Jeff could hear the men scrabbling closer. He slid around to the front of the rock which towered above him. The base was the problem. Three smaller rocks were forming a perfect wedge so in spite of its seemingly vulnerable position, while the wedge of smaller rocks was in place the large rock was virtually immovable.

The men below opened fire again and Jeff glanced down at them. If the rock were to topple they could not possibly avoid the avalanche that was bound to follow.

Jeff stared at the boulder where the enemy's bullets had blown small splinters from the face of it.

The idea germinated and steadily grew.

He needed the few shells he still had in his rifle, but he had plenty of .45 shells.

Keeping under cover, Jeff backed to the side of the boulder, put down the Winchester and drew both Colts. A drumroll of shots smashed into the smallest of the three rocks sending chips flying everywhere. Jeff studied the small boulder as he made a rapid reload. Again the guns set up their clamour.

The men below thought the shots were meant for them so they kept under cover.

Jeff heard the rock give what sounded like a groan as one side of it began to settle into the hollow created by the bullets. He snatched up his rifle and darted away from the rock as it tilted further and further. Then it stopped.

The men below were on the move, and once more bullets began searching for him.

Jeff had no more time to spare, with a curse of frustration he slipped behind the rock and began to climb, using its great height to protect him from the bullets.

He had climbed another twelve feet when some loose shale made him slip and he grabbed a small boulder to save himself. But it also began to move as the smaller stones beneath it slipped away. It crashed into his shoulder numbing his arm before crashing its way down the slope.

Spreadeagled as he was, and with a useless arm, he would be an easy target for the men behind him. He glanced desperately over his shoulder to see if they posed a threat.

He watched, fascinated as the small slide he had created rammed into larger rocks, increasing the momentum, sending them cascading towards the huge boulder.

There was another groan as the rock tilted even further. Then it was gone!

Jeff felt the earth tremble beneath him as the boulder crashed down the slope. He did not hear the frantic screams of the two men. The thunder of falling rocks was deafening. The dust cloud covered the slope until a vagrant gust of wind carried it away.

The boulders had been swept down into the narrow trail and it was almost completely blocked. Somewhere beneath it all were the men who had tried to kill him.

Jeff lay there for a while, dazed by the swift turn of events until the crackle of carbine fire reminded him of Luke on the other side of the hill.

He scrambled to his feet and climbed rapidly towards the ridge, the numbness gradually working out of his arm by the time he reached the top. Then he paused to study the lay of the land.

Most of the shooting was coming from a sloping section to his left. He counted four gunshots from that area.

There were two other men firing from directly below him and judging a point where the two angles would converge Jeff guessed that Luke was somewhere slightly to his right.

He waited for Luke's reply to the gunfire but his friend did not oblige.

Jeff was worried. The fact that Luke was not returning the fire meant either Luke was out of ammunition, he was injured or he did not want to reveal his hiding-place.

Jeff checked his Colts, the Winchester only contained nine cartridges, or was it eight? 'No time to check now,' he muttered, as he began moving swiftly down the slope towards where he assumed Luke to be.

21

Sanchos Alvarez had no idea who he was chasing; he knew they were not Mexicans by their headgear and that was good enough reason for him.

He was sure that Mason had been close when he ran from the Kyle farmstead and Sanchos had good reason to know that Mason would never give up. 'So be it,' he muttered, as he pressed his new *vaqueros* into the chase.

When he reached the two branches of the trail he directed the smaller band into the right hand one while he, with the remainder, chose the left.

The fugitive had led them a merry chase through the rocks until they had come upon the discarded horse. Sanchos had directed his men to search and kill anyone they found without delay.

Even as they were dismounting, however, two rifle shots claimed two men, the speed and accuracy making Sanchos believe the hunted man was indeed Mason, but with so many men at his disposal how could he lose!

He drove the men forward with lavish promises of a reward. 'Overwhelm him *muchachos*,' he shouted. 'He is but one man, he cannot defend himself against so many.'

Another of his men fell beside him, making Sanchos dive for shelter while he urged his men to greater efforts.

They had driven their quarry further and further into the wildness of the rocky area.

After a flurry of shots from his companions Sanchos heard a sudden curse of pain.

The Mexican's spirits rose. 'He is wounded; after him, after him *muchachos*,' he shouted excitedly. But although the fugitive had not fired again his men had not found him.

The superstitions were beginning to

eat at Sanchos once more. It seemed that no matter how many circling movements his men made in order to trap their victim the bird had always flown.

Then suddenly there were two shots. Another of his men died and still there was no sign of his enemy.

With just six of his men left Sanchos was beginning to have severe doubts, but he directed two to cut across the bottom of the rocks while the other four advanced from the side. 'We will force him up the hillside *muchachos*,' he told them. 'See, up there we have open ground, he will have no place to hide from us, go now, keep driving him upwards . . . '

* * *

Jeff moved swiftly down the slope, he had to pinpoint where Luke had gone to ground. He crouched, and allowed the sobbing wolf call to echo over the hillside. Jeff guessed that if Luke was alive he'd answer.

There was complete silence following the call. Jeff knew the Mexicans would be wondering how the call could come from the top of the ridge when they were closing in on an area much further down.

Moments later Luke imitated the call.

Jeff grinned tightly as he thought about Sanchos. 'What's he gonna make of that?' he murmured as he moved swiftly towards the two directly below him, aiming to bypass Luke's position.

The carbines set up their snapping racket again and Jeff noted that Luke was not replying. Probably moving to confuse the hunters, Jeff thought as he descended swiftly.

There was a rattle of loose rock followed by a curse as one of the Mexicans stumbled.

Jeff ghosted behind a rock and waited. The two men were very close, he could hear their heavy breathing and mumbled curses as they stumbled towards him. They were making no effort to be quiet.

'I did not plan for this kind of thing, Pablo,' grumbled one.

'Nor I,' replied Pablo. 'I expected to chase cows not kill men. I do not like this either.'

Jeff slid around the rock. The two men were resting, staring at the climb ahead.

'Don't turn around *amigos*,' Jeff told them quietly. 'It will be the last thing you ever do.'

The two men stiffened in shock but did not move.

'You would be very wise to lay down your guns now, and leave this place. If you do not you will die, and for a man who is not worthy of your sacrifice.'

The men showed no hesitation in divesting themselves of their weapons, and afterwards allowed themselves to be searched before hurrying off, eager to be gone.

Jeff threw the guns into the rocks. He was conscious of the continuing rattle of carbine fire higher up the slope. The tempo had increased but there was no answering shots from Luke.

Jeff climbed swiftly, the gunfire giving him a guide, and he was soon close enough to hear people moving around on the loose shale.

Deliberately he avoided the immediate area of the gunfire, aiming to circle around the spot so that he could be sure he was behind Luke's position. The last thing he wanted was to be caught between Luke and the *vaqueros*.

Jeff had paused for a moment to take stock of the situation when a Mexican clutching a carbine moved in front of him, his eyes fixed on a spot somewhere ahead.

Almost without thought Jeff placed the muzzle of his rifle in the back of the man's neck. 'Don't move *amigo*, don't even breathe,' he whispered. 'Put the gun on the ground, slowly and quietly.'

The man did as he was told. 'Now, take off your sombrero and pass it back to me then lie down on your face with your hands behind your back,' Jeff directed quietly.

Again the man carried out the instructions, and Jeff quickly cut the leather chin straps from the sombrero.

With one piece he tied the man's thumbs together, wrapping the remainder around the wrists. He tied the man's legs with the second piece. Then, pulling off the Mexican's bandanna he wrapped it around his mouth before rolling him between two large boulders.

Jeff drew his Colt and pointed it at the man's head. 'One sound *muchacho, comprende?*'

The man nodded vigorously.

'Obey and I will release you later.'

Jeff eased himself past a second large boulder . . . straight into Luke's cocked rifle.

'You almost died twice,' Luke croaked. 'Never heard a body make so much noise in my life.'

Jeff dropped to his knees. 'You hurt bad, Luke?'

'Some.' The faded grin changed to a

twist of pain. 'Tagged me twice, but I'll live, I'm out of shells too.'

'So what's with the rifle?'

'Bluff, son, just bluff. Figgered I could stop somebody blowing my stupid head off if they thought I had a loaded gun on 'em.'

Jeff handed Luke his rifle. 'Eight or nine shots in it, Luke; you hold the fort. It's time fer Colts now, they'll be comin' in soon, you ready?'

'How do I know if it's eight or nine?' grumbled Luke. 'Just my luck to pick a man who can't count.'

'You'll know when it's empty, it'll go click click click,' replied Jeff with a grim smile as he checked his Colts. 'Here we go.'

Jeff slipped into the surrounding rocks moving swiftly towards the remaining three men.

They were hurrying across a small clearing when Jeff stepped out in front of them.

The men were stunned into immobility and it gave him all the edge he needed. His guns were in his hands before any of the three could even begin to bring their carbines to bear. 'Don't even blink!' Jeff told them evenly. 'There's been enough killing.'

The three men hesitated; they knew that before any of them could swing their carbines at least one or two of them could be dead and no one wanted to be first in line.

Their faces revealed their indecision so Jeff pressed his advantage.

'If you try, my *amigo* in the rocks will also be ready to kill. He will now fire a shot into the air to prove this is so.'

As he finished speaking Luke responded by firing the rifle.

'If you place all your guns on the ground you may walk away unharmed. Your new employer is not worth your lives.'

The men glanced at each other, still hesitant.

Jeff thumbed back the hammers of both Colts. The sound was both loud and ominous. 'Decide now!' His voice deliberately held a note of finality.

'You give us your word?' queried one hesitantly.

'What have you to lose?' There was no compromise in Jeff's voice.

One after the other they threw down their carbines and pistols; knives quickly followed, then they waited, eyeing Jeff fearfully.

'Is that everything?'

They nodded, each looking to the other for confirmation.

'Very well; there is another of your *compadres* in the rocks yonder, untie him and leave. Remember, if you return for any reason, there will be no second chance. This is a day you've had given you, do not waste it, go in peace.'

The men backed slowly away murmuring their thanks, still unable to believe their luck as they suddenly turned and ran into the protection of the rocks.

Jeff lowered the hammers on his Colts and snugged them into the cut-away holsters as he trudged tiredly back to the niche where Luke was still lying.

'That was some speech you-all made to the opposition,' husked Luke. 'Figgered you was gonna take all day.'

Jeff could see by the greyness of his skin that Luke was not nearly as perky as he was trying to pretend. A quick examination of his wounds made Jeff realize just how bad they were. He'd taken a bullet through the thigh and another in the upper arm and he'd lost a considerable amount of blood.

Jeff slipped Luke's bandanna from around his neck and managed to stop the bleeding in the arm. Then he stripped off his own shirt. Ripping it into long strips and pads he started to bandage Luke's thigh but, as he tried to draw the two ends together, he found they were just too short. After a moment's hesitation he slipped his own bandanna from his neck and used it to join the two ends together.

Luke saw the rope and knife scars for the first time. 'Holy Jesus!' he muttered.

'No wonder you want Sanchos!'

Jeff stared into his eyes. 'So?'

'There's a time fer law, and a time fer jungle law, son,' muttered Luke. 'I'd say jungle law was about right.'

Jeff nodded curtly and continued to tie off the bandaging. 'Ain't much more I can do here, Luke. Looks like I'm gonna have to carry you to your hoss. You know, if you hadn't stuffed yourself so full of beans back there you'd take a lot less carryin'; you sure are a burdensome *hombre* to have around, feller,' grinned Jeff, as he stepped back to take a good look at his friend . . .

22

Sanchos could not believe what had happened, — his men had gone! Once again he was left alone.

Guns were useless against Mason; he had proved it in the past, and now, even with all the men he had hired Mason was still unharmed. His mind churned on driving him insane with hatred. How could he kill this man? Yet Sanchos knew he must find a way.

His hand brushed against his machete, so sharp, so keen, and he was an expert with it! Surely nothing could live if it did not have a head, and his machete, stoned so fine that it could be used as a razor, could take a man's head off with but a single stroke. Surely then this must be the way to rid himself forever of El Diablo! Sanchos was not worried about the other man, he was a mere nothing.

His state of mind was such that he had convinced himself that his destiny was to kill the man he hated more than any other.

Sanchos had spent some time crawling over rocks to place himself in the best attacking position. He now stood above the two men as he overheard Mason tell his friend that he would carry him to his horse. Sanchos waited until Jeff Mason had lifted the wounded man over his shoulder, then he jumped from the high rock, crashing down upon the two men.

Luke yelled his agony as he blacked out, while Jeff was knocked sprawling, his guns slipping from the holsters as he rolled over a large boulder.

Sanchos dived upon him, screaming like a demon. He was a strong man. Grabbing Jeff by his hair, he dragged him backwards as he raised the machete to strike.

Ignoring the drag on his hair Jeff raised both hands in a desperate effort to stop the descending blade. It took all his strength to stop the blow; using a double grip to twist the wrist he managed to deflect the wicked-looking blade.

Sanchos released Mason's hair in order to use both hands, trying to force the blade into his opponent's throat. In doing so Sanchos brought his face close to Jeff's. Instinctively Jeff flicked his head forward, smashing his forehead into the Mexican's nose with enough force to split it.

For a second the blow weakened Sanchos as he pulled away from the force of it.

Almost without thought Jeff's hand flicked to his neck where that paper-thin knife nestled in its soft leather sheath. It slid neatly into his hand, and in the same quick movement the arm straightened into a solid forward thrust.

The knife buried itself hilt deep into the Mexican's throat.

Sanchos stiffened, eyes widening in a stare of disbelief which slowly faded as the life drifted out of them.

Jeff pushed the man from him with a heavy sigh. At last it was over and Sanchos Alvarez had paid with his life.

Jeff climbed tiredly to his feet.

'You OK?' asked Luke.

'As I'll ever be,' replied Jeff, as he collected his Colts.

'We've still got to get out of here.'

'I know, and I've still got to carry you,' grumbled Jeff as he lifted Luke on to his shoulder. 'Oh, an' by the way,' he grunted as he began to stagger through the rocks. 'You owe me for a new shirt, fella, I don't supply free bandages to any old tramp I happen to meet.'

THE END